I REWIRED MY BRAIN:
MY JOURNEY TO FREEDOM

I REWIRED MY BRAIN:
MY JOURNEY TO FREEDOM

DR. KAY VONNE CASON-TURNER

SBPC

SIMMS BOOKS PUBLISHING CORPORATION

SBPC

SIMMS BOOKS PUBLISHING CORP.
Publishers Since 2012

Published By Simms Books Publishing
Jonesboro, GA

Copyright © Dr. Kay Vonne Cason-Turner, 2022
All rights reserved. No part of this book may be reproduced, scanned, or distributed in any print or electronic form without permission. Please do not participate in or encourage piracy of copyrighted materials in violation of the author's rights. Purchase only authorized editions.

Library of Congress Cataloging in Publication Data

2021922172

Dr. Kay Vonne Cason-Turner

I Rewired My Brain: My Journey to Freedom

ISBN: 978-1-949433-32-6

Printed in the United States of America
Edited by Mary Hoekstra
Cover by: Nidia Roman, RomanArts

Table of Contents

Acknowledgements i
Foreword iii
Introduction v
Chapter 1 Freedom: My Current Situation 1

PART 1
MY BACKSTORY: BONDAGE AND BREAKING FREE

Chapter 2 Beginnings 5
Chapter 3 The Continuation: Abuse and Trauma 12
Chapter 4 Momma No, Please Don't Shoot 24
Chapter 5 Marriage: Abuse, Abuse and More Abuse 36
Chapter 6 Depressed and Hopeless (911) 37
Chapter 7 The Great Escape (With a Message) 41
Chapter 8 The Hopeful Return 43
Chapter 9 Another Departure 45
Chapter 10 I Still Want My Family 46
Chapter 11 Enough 48
Chapter 12 A Blessing in Disguise 49
Chapter 13 My Church Experience 52
Chapter 14 Let's Try Church Again 60
Chapter 15 My Brain Rewiring 62

PART 2
THE JOURNEY OF CHANGE

Time To Get In The Driver's Seat....................65
Introduction 67
Chapter 16 Your Journey Begins 79
Chapter 17 Unconscious Choices and Habits 81
Chapter 18 How We Develop Habits 84
Chapter 19 You Can Change: Rewire Your Brain 86
Chapter 20 Programs as Belief Systems 88
Chapter 21 Triggers 91
    Situational Triggers
    Thoughts as Triggers
Chapter 22 Thought/Feeling Connection 96
Chapter 23 Reticular Activating System 99
Chapter 24 Strategize to Rewire Your Brain 105
Chapter 25 Affirmations 108
Chapter 26 Vision Boards 110
Chapter 27 Meditation 115
Chapter 28 Visualization 121
Chapter 29 Mindfulness 123
Chapter 30 Reinterpreting Your Past 127
Chapter 31 Identify and Change Your Programs 132
Chapter 32 How Long Will It Take to Rewire My Brain 134
Chapter 33 Positive Support System 139
Chapter 34 Conscious Effort: Investing Your Time and Energy Into Yourself 144

Acknowledgements

First, I would like to thank my "Bonus sister" Lee-Ann Hampton for consistently being on me about getting this book out soon. She has had my manuscript two years prior to its' publication, and she said it's now roughed up from the numerous times of her reading, re-reading, making notes, spreading out the pages, and constantly having to shuffle them back together to fit back into the envelope where she keeps it.

She had been contacting me saying "get this book out soon, people need this book." She said it's her "go-to" when those growth-promoting situations arise. Lee-Ann thank you for your insistent nudging, all of your encouragement, and your heartfelt suggestions. I finally did it. I REWIRED MY BRAIN is now available to other people besides you.

I also want to thank my daughter Britney for her passion and desire that my endeavors be exceptional. Rain or shine, tired or fully-energized, throughout the process of completing this book, she was always there to offer support, share ideas, and provide treasured feedback.

Additionally, my special thanks to my family and friends for their invaluable assistance that contributed to the final outcome of this book and the complimentary workbook.

Further, I want to thank my husband for stopping what he was doing to listen to my ideas and for kindly dealing with late dinners, delivered meals, my manuscript all over the living room, and my spontaneous disappearances into my work area, whenever I had a my "aha" moments for this project. Much love and appreciation to you!

Most important, Thank you, God, The Creator. Thank you for my journey. I would not change anything, as it has led to me being the woman I am today. Because of my journey, I have gained great knowledge and wisdom. This has enabled me to be a guide and a source of enlightenment to others.

Foreword

I Rewired My Brain, My Journey to Freedom is more than just a book. It's a blueprint to a new life. It will give you the step-by-step approach to becoming the highest vision of yourself. This book will help you break the chains of the habits and traits that hold you in mental and emotional bondage.

When you follow the blueprint, applying the tools and strategies with consistency, you optimize your ability to obtain your desired end result. Your outcome will be in alignment with what you choose for yourself, even in the midst of your trials and tribulations.

Dr. Kay Vonne Cason-Turner's testimony of her evolutionary life journey to freedom is evidence that a greater experience of life is possible despite a history of hardships. I have known Dr. Cason-Turner for over 30 years. We met when she was going through some of the darkest hours of her life. I was a witness to her tireless search and acquisition of knowledge and commitment to her inner work that ultimately gave birth to the woman that she is today. She went through the process of successfully rewiring her brain. Now, she helps others to rewire their brain so that they, too, can experience the triumphant freedom that it engenders.

I would like to encourage and inspire others to read this life-changing book. Dr. Cason-Turner's life story is page-turning. The knowledge and wisdom that she presents is transformative. It is my hope, that after you read her gripping story, you make the decision to take your own journey to freedom, and break your chains of mental and emotional bondage.

Godis aka Aldonna

Introduction

Rewiring our brain is how we experience long-lasting, as opposed to short-term change. It can produce the kind of change that will transform our life. There comes a time in life when we all need to make a change. We might need to change our behavior, our mindset, belief systems, a relationship, and even our surroundings. As our lives unfold, one day to the next, one year to the next, change becomes necessary. Life demands it. Holding on to what is familiar, maintaining our same habits that are not productive, will only lead to distress, destruction, and even devastation. I write this not only from my knowledge as a Psychologist. I write this from personal experiences.

I wrote this book because I have a desire to help people to change their life. This book not only contains the tools and processes that I utilized to rewire my brain; this book also contains my own personal journey. As you follow my journey, you may find that you took some of the same roads – good and not-so-good – that I followed. You may find that your journey, like mine contained significant life altering elements that were beyond your control.

Other people, their circumstances, and their choices influenced the way that your journey unfolded; nevertheless, you as did I, responded to our life challenges with the insight or lack thereof that we had at that time. We responded to life based upon however our brain was programmed. If we "really" knew better, we would do better, hence, as our journey of life unfolded, we did the best that we knew to do.

As I grew in wisdom and insight, I did better. I made more productive choices. My life changed and eventually transformed. I became a better version of myself as I gained a significant level of freedom from my own programming (how my brain was wired). Because I have dedicated my life to helping others, I wanted to go back and assist others in becoming as liberated and fulfilled as I have become. I wanted to help others to rewire their brain.

It is my hope, that after you read this book, you will realize that no matter what you have gone through in your life, there is still hope for you. You too, can rewire your brain. No matter where you go, there you are; you and your thoughts, belief systems and behaviors. When you rewire your brain, you empower yourself by changing your negative or unproductive habitual ways of thinking and behaving. You also change unproductive belief systems. Rewiring your brain empowers you to live your life more consciously. Rewiring your brain will open you up to an entirely new level of awareness. If you are reading this book, it's time for you to go to your next level up. Embrace the process of your transformation. Rewire Your Brain!

Chapter 1

Freedom: My Current Situation

Here I sit, on the balcony of my high-rise, luxury apartment off the water, with the sun on my face, drinking a chilled glass of chardonnay, and looking at my boat down in the marina. I'm reminiscing on my travels around the world…Paris, London, Italy, Greece, Thailand, China three times, Hong Kong, Africa, the Bahamas, Jamaica, Aruba, Mexico, Nice, Monaco, Monte Carlo and more. I loved them all.

I have enjoyed shopping sprees all over the world and have a wardrobe that I love. My closets are like a store, outfits, shoes and boots to match. Of course, I have some select designer handbags. I love cruising in my Mercedes, smooth-riding, on my way to my office.

I'm a psychologist (PsyD), and I own an outpatient mental health private practice wherein I love helping all of my patients: Children, teens, women, men, and families challenged by anxiety, depression and the distress of separation or divorce.

I really cherish and enjoy my family life. After writing this book I got married to my husband, who was my childhood sweetheart during middle school. Further, I love my sons and daughter who are intelligent and deep-thinking individuals with whom I enjoy interacting, and my beautiful grandchildren really make my heart sing. I embrace Love, Peace and Harmony every day. I experience a sense of joy with which I've been richly blessed. I have a close and personal relationship with God, who has assisted and guided me in my journey of inner growth and transformation.

As beautiful as my life is, everything is not perfect, however, I continue to move forward, growing, and changing those things that I can change.

I want you to know that my life was not always like this. This life I now live was once merely a figment of my imagination. It was once a dream, now made manifest, a vision that I nurtured as I did everything, I learned to do to make it a reality.

Now that you know my current story, I want to share my journey of how I got here. I rewired my brain.

PART 1
MY BACKSTORY: BONDAGE AND BREAKING FREE

Chapter 2

Beginnings

I have no memory of my parents living together since they separated and divorced before I was 4 years old. My older sister and I lived with my mother and visited my father about every other weekend. My dad was a barber who owned his own barbershop; my mother worked in a bank until she leveled up financially and started working at the auto factory with my uncles.

By the time I was 7 years old, from my memory, my mother had become a "functioning" alcoholic and she was mentally and emotionally abusive toward me. And if that wasn't bad enough, I was being molested by "step" family members who were all just a little older than me.

Further, I was bullied in school and bullied at home by my older sister. It seemed that my older sister didn't like me, just because I was born. Later, when I was older, I could see reasons why she didn't like me.

I used to unintentionally destroy her toys (her big doll named Susie got a haircut by yours truly, her glass Alice in Wonderland figurine shattered in a race down my basement stairs with all my other dolls who participated, and her jumping Mr. Potato Head™ stopped jumping.) You get my point. I used to break so many things that Aunt Glady, my favorite aunt, nicknamed me destructive Annie.

Okay, getting back to my sister not liking me. My sister used to punch my arm when no adults were around, and tell me that she hated me. She often did this after I would "perform" during the family celebrations at the request of all of the adults who liked to watch me dance.

I was that kid who danced with a serious face and my tongue sticking out. The adults used to geek me up by yelling, "Get it, Get it." I had a mean robot dance and I was a hit with the Popcorn Dance. After my "award-winning" performances, I used to feel so happy and excited until, like I mentioned earlier, my sister would punch me, say she hated me, and then I would cry.

By the time I got a little older, let's say around middle school, we would bicker like normal sisters and she didn't punch me anymore, because I grew to be very close to her height and weight. That doesn't mean that she stopped being aggressive towards me. When we argued, she would throw things at me. I can remember a few times when she threw a glass ashtray my way. I ducked. She missed. We had some good times and some not so good times.

As for my mom, even though she was an alcoholic, she was a great provider, making sure that we had everything that we needed and more. My mother took me and my sister to the beauty shop/hair salon every other week to get our hair done. She bought our clothes from Lord & Taylor™, Hudsons™ and Sax Fifth Avenue™. She used to pay for me to have specially made shoes at Hudsons™ because I had wide feet and the in-stock shoes were too tight.

My mother sent me and my sister to charm school and she paid for my sister to be in a program to become a debutante (my Aunt Gladie's influence). My mother bought me and my sister dolls that crawled, walked, talked, peed, and grew hair.

She made sure that we had the best of everything, because her mother had died when she was only 2 years old, and that led to her having a hard life. When my mother's mother died, she was staying with some older people who took on the task of raising her. My mother thought those were her biological parents until my mom was about 7 years old. At that time, a lady who lived next door got into an argument with the family raising my mother, and that lady told my mother that her mother had died when she was 2 years old.

My mother was devastated because she thought the older people were her mother and father. Shortly thereafter, those older people, whose last name was Grey, had marital issues and gave my mother to some people down the street. Then they eventually gave my mother to someone else. And this went on for years.

My mother was in a girls' home at some point, and she also suffered abuse. This haunted my mother to her core.

I remember times during my childhood when my mother used to get drunk and cry, saying, "I was thrown from pillow to post, nobody wanted me; nobody loved me." My mother talked about times when she was treated very badly as a child. When I asked for details, she said that she did not want to talk about it.

She never healed from her childhood wounds. My mother's alcoholism was her way of self-medicating. To be certain, due to her not feeling loved and valued, and because she did not heal, she did not really love or value herself. She had issues showing emotional love to me, and she had issues valuing me as a "being." Hence, while her "love language" was being the great provider that she was, she was not very nurturing towards me and she was downright mean most of the time when she was drinking alcohol.

For much of my childhood, on about four or five of the days of each week, my mother yelled at me, telling me that I was "dumb and stupid, with no common sense." She'd yell that I was "never going to amount to sh*t." I used to cry in devastation from my emotional pain.

As I got a little older, I started yelling back at her, crying, in my defense proclaiming, "I am going to be something, I am, I am going to be something." She even said that she wished that she had never had me. Also, my mother used to tell me that I didn't deserve anything.

The emotional environment in which I grew up was too often negative, unsupportive and degrading. Hurt people, hurt people! My mother was hurting and she ended up hurting me. She frequently told me, "Life is hard; when you make your bed, you've got to lie in it."

I think that the best thing that my mother did tell me was to be independent. She added that I would not be able to depend on anybody, so I needed to learn how to take care of myself. And she always said, "Where there is a will, there is a way!"

Up to this point in my backstory, as just a young child, my brain was already downloading a lot of negative programs. Maybe you can relate to this list, too:

- I was dumb and stupid with no common sense and would never amount to sh*t
- I'm not valuable
- I don't deserve anything
- I can't depend on anybody
- I don't matter
- I wasn't wanted
- Life is hard
- When you make your bed, you have got to lie in it

- My mother and sister are mean and they don't love or like me
- I'm a victim

Fortunately, I did have support and I received good messages from my dad and my Aunt Gladie whenever I saw them. My father and my Aunt Gladie used to tell me that I could be anything that I wanted to be, and my dad used to tell me that I was brilliant, just like him. :)

Chapter 3

The Continuation: Abuse and Trauma

Now that I have provided a glimpse of the emotional climate in my home when I was a young child, I will take you a little further and into the part of my backstory where the sexual abuse resides.

Unfortunately, sexual abuse was a big part of my backstory. I was sexually abused from approximately age 5 or 6 years old, into my early 20s. Some of the details I provide here shine the light on how my brain got programmed via some of those experiences. I also identify which of the previously identified programs were activated and operating.

The sexual abuse all started when I was molested by stepfamily members who were a little older than me. I do understand that we were kids then, and we are all adults now. I hold no negative judgments towards them; however, they are part of my story.

At night while I was sleeping, the boys would get in the bed with me, one at a time, and then fondle and hump on me. When I would wake up to this happening, they would tell me to be quiet and not tell anyone. I was scared so I didn't say anything.

As time went on, eventually, this turned into them fondling and humping on me during daylight hours when we were playing together and no one else was around. I still didn't tell anyone.

One day, my sister walked in on them sexually abusing me and she told me that I was nasty for letting it happen. I felt ashamed. I felt a sense of guilt. She obviously didn't tell my parents, because no adults ever approached me about it.

Even though I was never threatened, I was still afraid, and now ashamed to say anything. So the sexual abuse continued. When it happened at night, I learned to lie there as if I was still sleeping. When it happened during the daytime, I froze. I used to go away in my mind and come back when they were done. I later learned that I was dissociating.

I got very good at dissociating, especially when the older

teenage family members came over and started doing the same things to me.

It is important to note that these perpetrators of sexual abuse were always very nice to me; I lived at home with an alcoholic mother who was mentally and emotionally abusive, and with a sister who seemed to not like me. The abuse by these family members went on from the time I was about 5 years old to 10 years old. As my story unfolds, unfortunately, you'll see that the abuse worsened.

I had been abused so often as a young child that by the age of 6 or 7 years old, I sexually abused my cousin who was approximately 2 years younger than me. I also was sexually inappropriate with some of my female friends who had also been sexually abused. We called it "being nasty."

Moving forward with my story, when I was 10 to 11 years old, I was molested by a man (maybe 40 years old or older) who owned a jewelry store.

That situation started like this: One day, I was walking home from school and I stopped and went into a jewelry store. The owner of the jewelry store was a man who was very nice to me. He started to "groom" me by allowing me to choose any jewelry that I wanted and he also gave me money for candy and ice cream (I didn't even need money, my mother always made sure I had enough). When I got ready to go home, he would always smile and ever so nicely tell me to come back, and I always did. Sometime after my third visit, he asked me if I wanted to see the rest of the store.

Of course, as a curious little girl, I said yes. After all, he was so nice to me. So he took me behind the curtains in the back and showed me around. What happened next was unthinkable. He lifted me up and sat me on a counter, he spread my legs open, and fondled and grinded (with his pants on) my private areas, and kissed all over my neck and chest. (It was grossing me out as I wrote about it. This man was sick!)

As distorted as this situation was and is, this man said nice things to me, he used to make me smile, laugh and feel happy. However, when he was abusing me, I felt very nervous and uncomfortable, so I would freeze and dissociate until it was over. But when I came back from my inner journey (wherever I went), my interactions with this abuser who manipulated me had a tendency to provoke within me feelings of significance, like I mattered, like I was valuable and important to him. I felt good and I felt shame and guilt, all jumbled together.

A little later, when I was about 12 years old, an adult family member molested me. This all came about with my first babysitting job. I felt proud to have a job. I used to babysit his children; I think it was during summer break. Anyway, at night, after I put the children to bed, I would fall asleep on the floor until he came home from work. Then, I would wake up to him getting on top of me and having his hands in my panties. I used to freeze and dissociate until it was over. I don't remember why, but after a year or two of this going on, I told my mother what was happening. She confronted him on the phone, and he and his wife said I was lying.

That babysitting job ended and I did not go to his house anymore, but while I was still babysitting, when I was 13 years old, my boyfriend was 21 years old. I agreed to engage in sexual acts, with much influence and pressure from him. He made me watch pornography with him and he used to tell me that I was a lady, that I should not do cartwheels up and down the street anymore, and that I should stand and act a certain way ("like a lady," when I was a 13-year-old kid). Anyway, I told my boyfriend about how that adult family member was sexually abusing me when I was babysitting the children, and my 21-year-old boyfriend tried to help out by driving me and the children to his house for me to babysit them there. This did not fly, as I was soon told by the children's parents that I had to babysit the children in their own home. So, I babysat them until I told my mother what was happening, and then the gig was up.

My boyfriend and I were happy about that, as this gave us the opportunity to spend more time together. When I was with my 21-year-old boyfriend, I felt loved, valued, cared for, and happy. He was very nice to me. He said that I was like a cute puppy and that he could never be mean to me. When he was at my house, he even had a way of talking to my mother when she was drunk and getting her in a good mood. He had learned how to deal with my alcoholic mother because he was raised by an alcoholic mother. This guy and I were together for around two years. He wanted to marry me. I asked my mother if I could marry him, and she hesitantly said yes. Shortly thereafter, he went to prison and I was devastated.

From my perspective, he was my way to happiness. To be certain, I was way too young for that guy, and I later found out that our sexual interactions were a crime, identified as statutory rape, but that "something" that seemed so good for me was so bad for me at the same time.

I continue with yet another episode of sexual abuse in my backstory: I was date-raped as a teenager, by a different adult in his 20's. He lived in the neighborhood and I used to see him all the time. He used to frequently ask me to go for a ride in his hot-rod car. I went for a ride with him one day and we went to Belle Isle.

It was dusk, he parked his car, and we talked. The music in his car was playing loud. He had a small piece of a joint that we smoked together, and shortly thereafter, he started to kiss me. He was trying to take it further, but I did not want that. He had laid on top of me and I told him to stop. I tried to push him off me, but he was too heavy and strong. I was too embarrassed and ashamed to scream or yell out for help. I froze and dissociated until it was over.

As the days went on, I told my mother and she told some neighbors. My mother had thoughts about prosecuting him and the neighbors said that they would go to court on his behalf because I was "fast" and I willingly got into his car. I felt more embarrassed and ashamed, because now other people in the neighborhood knew what happened and they blamed me. We never prosecuted and life went back to my "normal."

When I was 15 years old, I got pregnant by a man who eventually became my husband, now ex-husband. (There's more about the abuse I endured in that marriage later in the book.)

Anyway, at 15 years old, when I was pregnant, I was nervous about being a teenage mother, but I was looking forward to having a baby because I thought that I would have someone who would always love me. When I had my son, I was still in high school.

My child's father used to babysit our son while I went to school. He was 8 years older than me, and he was abusive physically, mentally, emotionally and sexually. When he would beat me up, I would break off the relationship, but in the morning, when I brought our baby to him (after walking six blocks, with our child in a stroller, rain, sleet, snow or hail), he would say he was not going to babysit unless I would be his girlfriend again and have sex with him. I loved school and I needed a babysitter, so I would stay in the relationship, and quickly have sex with him, so that I could get to school on time, while he watched our child. This happened many times.

Fortunately, I was very smart in school. I got "double promoted," two times and I was able to complete my high school education at 16 years old.

In my backstory of distress, there is another episode of sexual abuse. As if things had not already been bad enough, at 17 years old, I was raped, in my home, by an intruder. I was grabbed out of a deep sleep, pushed to the floor, bound, gagged, raped repeatedly, and held "hostage," for about 6 or 7 hours before he left. He demanded money and I didn't have any.

That night, I was terrified for my life and the life of my child, who slept through the entire ordeal. I initiated conversations with that man throughout the night (when the gag was not around my mouth). I called him an endearing term that one might call a friend, so that he might think of me as a friend and not kill me and my son. I guess it worked, because he loosened the fabric belt he had tied around my wrists when I told him that I could not feel my fingers, which had become numb. He also moved my son over on the couch, because he said that my son was almost on the edge where he could fall.

Throughout this horrifying situation, I was calm and continued to talk to him. Hearing the sound of his voice gave me some sense of where he was in my house. Near the end of this ordeal, things got quiet. He did not answer me. I called out to him to no avail. He did not respond. I listened closely and I did not hear him walking around; I called out to him again and again and he still did not answer. When I finally realized that he was likely gone, I wiggled out of the items he had used to blindfold me. I looked around and did not see him. I quickly wiggled out of the things he had used to tie me up. Then, I scooted myself over to the couch to check on my son. Thank God he was okay and still asleep.

Finally, I called Aunt Gladie. What a relief it was to hear her voice! She told me that she was on her way. She called the police and my mother, who was still at work. Aunt Gladie got to my house within 5 minutes, still in her pajamas and housecoat. By the time my mother got home, the house was surrounded by police, inside and out. Police dogs were in the house. There was white powder everywhere as they were dusting for fingerprints, to no avail. They never found him.

I suffered from some serious PTSD symptoms for a long time. I started sleeping with steak knives wherever I would sleep. I kept a steak knife under the couch cushion and a steak knife between the box-spring and mattress of my bed. I used to practice slowly grabbing it and pulling it out in a way to stab someone. I made sure that the knives were positioned exactly where I needed them.

Then, one morning, something happened that changed all that preparation. I was sound asleep on the couch, and my son, who was 1 year old at the time, was trying to wake me up. I was a very deep sleeper. Well, as I felt the presence of someone over me, touching me, I slowly moved my hand to the knife and grabbed it. Then as I was slowly pulling the knife from under the cushion, I became conscious enough to realize that it was my son. I was horrified at the fact that I could have killed him. I cried and I put all of the knives away. It brought tears to my eyes to even write about that incident with my son. That could have been a tragic moment!

Chapter 4

Momma No, Please Don't Shoot!

You're probably thinking that I should be up for a "break" in life by now. Not!

Also, when I was 17 years old, my mother was drunk, held a shotgun towards me, and told me that I had to get out. This ordeal happened one evening after I had gotten home from work. I was not feeling well that evening, so after picking up my son from his babysitter's house and coming home to my mother's house, I laid in the bed. While I was laying in the bed, my son wanted something to drink.

He kept coming to me, saying, "Momma, Momma, I'm thirsty, I'm thirsty." I kept telling him "Okay, in a minute."

To my surprise, while laying on my bed, I opened my eyes to my mother holding a shotgun on me. She said to me, in a slurred and drunken voice, "I brought you here and I will take you out." She complained about me not getting my son something to drink. She was so drunk and menacing as she continued to hold the gun on me. I was terrified! I slid back into a corner of my bed, grabbing pillows and putting them in front of me, so as to stop a bullet, I guess.

I was crying and begging, "Momma, no, Momma, no please don't shoot me." I was calling for her husband who was in the other room and telling him she had a gun and she was trying to shoot me.

Eventually, as my mother continued to brandish that gun at me, I slowly crawled toward the edge of the bed because I remembered that my telephone was on the floor. With tears streaming down my face, I calmly and slowly maneuvered my way to the edge of the bed to get to my telephone. Damn, it was right by my mother's feet. Slowly moving, crying, and begging her to not shoot me, while looking down the barrel of her gun, I slowly grabbed the telephone receiver to call, you guessed it, my favorite Aunt Gladie.

As I was dialing the number, on the rotary dial phone, my mother started yelling to her husband that I was calling the police. My mother's husband started to come towards my bedroom. It took him what seemed like a long time to get to my room, and when he finally got there, he grabbed the gun from my mother, saying, "I told you what to do a long time ago."

I still don't know what that meant. By this time, my Aunt Gladie had quickly come over to the house (She lived two blocks away). Aunt Gladie was yelling at my mother about pulling the gun on me. My mother told me that I had to get out that night. I started packing my and my son's belongings, and putting them into large green plastic garbage bags. I loaded them into my car until I had most of the things that I owned in there. I even packed up my box 11-inch black and white TV that sat on my nightstand.

I went over to my best friend's house; she was my son's godmother. Her mother allowed me to stay there for a couple of days, but then I had to leave, however, my son could stay.

Being grateful for that and with nowhere to really go, I drove around and found nice neighborhoods that appeared to be safe. Once I found a safe space, I would park my car, lean my seat back, with doors locked, and fall asleep. I was homeless for almost 1 week and ironically, because I used to love to go to Northland Skating Rink, when the next skating day came, I went skating, homeless and all.

Interestingly, I had just started skating with this guy that I met 2 weeks prior. He was a very nice, polite guy, close to my age, who just got out of the Army. When the skating session was over, he walked me to my car and he saw all of the bags and my TV in the backseat. He asked me what was going on and I told him that my mother had pulled a gun on me and put me out of the house and I was sleeping in my car.

He told me that I could come and stay at his house, where he lived with his mother and brother in the Herman Gardens projects. He talked to his mother, who was nice enough to let me and my son stay there until I could get my own place.

The guy and I became a couple. We had a lot of fun together and we continued couples' skating, doing all kinds of daring and cool moves. The guy and his mother were very nice to me and my son until I moved out.

Thus far in my backstory, there is definitely the element of my not feeling valued. This is truly evident with my history of sexual abuse. I did not feel loved and valued at home, so that made it very easy for older guys, for pedophiles, to target me, and "provide what I was missing," to feel loved and valued, to feel like I mattered, to feel I was wanted by someone.

This lack of being valued and feeling loved happens to a lot of children and teenagers. Maybe some of you can relate to that or identify your own backstory with those elements.

Heck, a lot of adults stay in unhealthy relationships because of a misperception that the person loves or values them, even though the relationship is unloving and toxic.

In addition, the abuse that I endured deepened my "victim consciousness," which left me with feelings of helplessness. It is important for me to note that the program of me being "dumb and stupid with no common sense" is also an element in my backstory.

To give you more clarity on this, when my mother used to say the "dumb and stupid" put down, a lot of times, she followed it up with a conversation about when I got older, I would know some of the things she was talking about, and it was true about some things she taught.

And she used to frequently say, "You are going out into the world, ass backwards," and that comment was associated with age, as well. Hence, you make poor choices ("ass backwards") when you are young and make better choices when you are older. In my thinking, since I was "dumb and stupid with no common sense," and I was going out into the world "ass backwards," and I had to go "out in the world," then I needed someone who was older, so that they could guide me.

After all, I was "dumb and stupid with no common sense" and was "never going to amount to sh*t." This constant programming, almost every day of the week, was a contributing factor to me making choices to be with older guys as my boyfriends, so they could guide me. I thought I was onto something. #NOT. That "dumb and stupid," "ass backwards" programming made me not trust myself. If I did feel like something was off, was it really?

That programming was so deeply wired into my brain that in my youth I used to have a recurring dream that there was a dangerous situation happening and everyone was running away from the danger, but I was running in slow motion toward the danger, trying to grab onto others so I would get pulled away from the danger. Those were some scary childhood dreams, dreams directly related to my programming!

Fortunately, those programs are no longer running in my life because I have rewired/reprogrammed my brain using the methods that I described in Part 2 of this book. I know that I am lovable, valuable, important, intelligent, and wise. I know that I deserve great things. I know that there is nothing "wrong" with me --I am a work in progress. I know that I am wanted and extremely important to others. I know that I am not a victim.

I no longer have a "victim consciousness." As a matter of fact, I am a survivor and a creator. I put in the necessary work to do my part in consciously creating my reality. Also, I know that if I make a poor choice, I can learn and grow from my mistakes. Life does not have to be identified as hard; "hard" is a perspective that causes distress. Life has challenges for us to move through.

We are evolving beings. I know, as long as I use every obstacle as an opportunity for growth, then my life is what I make it. I have learned how to turn lemons into lemonade and I am here to teach others how to do it.

Okay, I had to get that out; Period.

Returning to my backstory, what also can be detected is the programming of believing it was shameful and embarrassing to be abused; it was as if something was wrong with me, rather than the abusers being the people with the real problem.

It is truly sad that I was raped in a car on Belle Isle, and there were people who would have heard me if I'd cried out. But sadly, I was too embarrassed and felt ashamed, so I froze and dissociated, yet again.

During my journey of healing, I wrote a poem about my sexual abuse experiences as a child. It is in my book, *From Sexual Energy to Love: A Journey of Passion, Desire, Oneness and Healing.* Before I share the poem, I want to give you a backdrop to it for your understanding. Before my healing journey, I was always focused on the "next thing" that I had to deal with.

I had some serious issues that were constantly in my path, so I was trying to put those fires out as best I could. When I got to a safe place in my life, free from abuse, my healing began. In a setting when I was getting in contact with my "inner child," so I could move forward with my healing and my desired life, my "inner child" spoke to me through my poem:

Did You Ever Cry for Me?

No one was there to care
No one was there to share
My hurt, my pain, my shame
That I eventually attached to my name

No protection for a little girl
Wandering in a dark, cold world

While I tried to do my best
I often wandered into predators' nests

I usually froze myself in fear
As the violators came near

Too scared to try and break free
No one around to save me

My quickest exit was out of my mind
True peace I tried to find

When it was time, then I would come back
And try to keep up my act
Will you ever come back for me?
I need safety and security

I know that this one thing is true
I really, really do need you!

I cried as this poem came through me and onto the page. Then I told my inner child that I would keep her safe, protect her, and let her know that I love her. As a result of my inner work, I have healed/reprogrammed my brain and now I live as an empowered woman.

***An important note relative to anyone whose parent has done something awful to you: If you are an adult and you have unresolved childhood issues related to some things your parents did or didn't do, there is nothing that you can do to change the past, other than reinterpreting the meaning of what happened in the past.

If you want to be happy, experience inner peace, it will be important for you to deal with the programs that get triggered when you are in the presence of your parents, having a conversation about them, or if your parents are mentioned in a conversation that you overhear.

Your parents did all that they knew to do, given the programs, information and perspectives that they had to work with at that time.

Currently, if you are looking for something "wrong" about your parents so you can continue justifying why you're holding on to your anger or hurt, you will find it, because they are not perfect and neither are you.

As an adult, your programs are your responsibility. If your programs are not bringing you joy, taking you where you want to go in life, it is on you to change your programs, to rewire your brain. No one can do this for you. You can't level up and move forward if you are holding on to a past that is bringing you down. In order to move forward, you have to leave the past in the past, where it belongs, or reinterpret it.

Take a moving forward step now. Liberate yourself. Rewire your brain.

Chapter 5

Marriage: Abuse, Abuse and More Abuse

When I was around 20 years old, I married my son's father. He beat me up the day before the wedding and I was too embarrassed to call it off, so I married him anyway. The beatings continued after we got married (not on the wedding day). A couple of years into our marriage, one day he beat me up, and I was tired of this. When I got the chance, I got away from him. I grabbed my keys that were nearby, ran out the back door, and jumped in my car. I locked the car doors, turned the car on. He came out the back door and I had a vision of his red blood, all over the back of the house. He was standing in the perfect spot for my vision to become a reality. I quickly put the car in gear and hit the accelerator, hard! Just so happened, the car was in neutral. He hurriedly put bricks behind my tires. I could not move the car.

I waited in the car for a long time. Damn, it was getting late and I finally had to get out. So I did. I got out of the car, went inside the house, he heard me come in, and he beat me up again, this time for trying to run him over with the car.

Chapter 6

Depressed and Hopeless (911)

During another episode, I went through what felt like emotional torture, while I was nursing my black eye and swollen lip. It all started after another beating. There I was, sitting on the commode in the bathroom, nursing my wounds. In walks my husband with his sawed-off shotgun. He pointed that thing at me and said, "Hehe haha you don't know if it has bullets in it," as he pressed the shotgun against my forehead, then my temple, then close to the back of my head, then to my other temple and then back to my forehead. Then, he repeated over and over again, "Stand up, sit down, stand up, sit down." I followed his commands, standing up and sitting down on the commode, in tears, crying, afraid. I feared for my life!

During those days, back in the 80's, I used to call the police sometimes, and when they came, he would have already left the house. One time, he stayed, and when they questioned him, he sat on the couch with his feet on the coffee table and said, "I didn't touch her."

Sometimes I would have black eyes and a swollen lip, and sometimes not, because after a while, I learned to run to a corner and hide my face. He had been telling me that he was going to beat me so bad that no one else would want me.

He used to also tell me that he would kill me if I left him. He said that if he couldn't have me, no one could. After many black eyes and swollen lips, whenever he began to attack me, I started running and facing a corner and squatting down to protect my face and teeth. When I squatted, I put my head by my knees, while he was hitting me.

Getting back to the police, they never arrested him. They said that it was my word against his. Well, the day after he pointed that sawed-off shotgun at me, I felt so depressed, helpless, hopeless, powerless and in despair that I went into the bathroom, opened the cabinet and got a bottle of ibuprofen. I emptied a lot of pills into my hands, I put a lot of them into my mouth, and I drank some water to swallow them.

I stayed in the bathroom, while silently crying. After a while, I got scared about what I had done and I called and told my sister.

My sister called and told my husband. My sister also called 911 and told them what happened but would not give them my name or address. The operator told my sister to get me some syrup of ipecac, which would make me vomit. She told my husband, he rushed to the store, got the syrup, and brought it home for me to take. I took it and vomited a lot. He cried and told me how sorry he was, how much he loved me, and that he would never do it again. Actually, he did this frequently, the tears and apologies.

After that grueling day, life went on and so did the beatings. I used to call my mother and sister, crying and screaming after the beatings until they told me not to call them anymore. They said that since I wasn't going to leave him, don't call them because my calls were too distressing. So I stopped calling and the beatings continued. I wrote a poem about how I felt during the time in my life that I was being beaten. The name of the poem is "I Feel."

I Feel

I feel no hope
And not much pain

Just numb existence
Is this not sane

To feel is good
To feel is bad

To feel is inevitable
It's happy, it's sad

Take a look inside
Consider what's real
It's not a hoax
You feel what you feel.

Chapter 7

The Great Escape (With a Message)

On one occasion, while I was at my mother's house, Aunt Gladie talked to me about the abuse in my marriage. She said, "Get out of there. He's going to kill you!" I cried and said okay. She called my uncles in Texas and arranged for me and my son to live there with them.

I secretly made my plan. I had started saving the money that my husband gave me to pay the bills, so I could buy Greyhound bus tickets for me and my son, then 4 years old, to go to Texas. I also kept money to have some pocket change.

I think my Aunt Gladie and my mother might have given me some money to help out, but I don't remember. For my escape, before I left home with my son, I got magic markers and wrote in big letters all over the living room and kitchen walls I HATE YOU. When the black marker ran out, I got a red one. I wrote these three words everywhere; I HATE YOU. I even went down into my husband's music studio in the basement. He had several keyboards and synthesizers in the studio that he loved. I took my time and wrote a letter on each key to every keyboard; I HATE YOU.

When there were no more keys to write on, I went back upstairs. As I was walking toward the front door with my son, and our luggage, I opened the door, and I turned and looked back. I saw the writing on the wall -- literally and figuratively -- and I knew that it was time to go. We walked out, and I closed that door.
Until I opened it again.

Chapter 8

The Hopeful Return

Yeppers, that's right, I opened that door again. I was in Texas for close to a year and things were going well. Initially, my husband didn't know where I was, because my sister would not tell him when he called and cried to her. I was keeping it secret as well. Then one day, after so much time had gone by, I decided to call him. He cried and apologized and told me how much he loved me and wanted me to come home. He said that he would never put his hands on me again. There were many phone calls and many tears between us.

Eventually, I decided to go back to Detroit, so I left Texas and went back home. Things were going well. I got pregnant with our second child after 2 years of no beatings. After that, the beatings started again.

Fast forward: When I was around 6 to 8 months pregnant with our last son, child number 3, my husband beat me up. I was on the floor with him on top of me, trying to get up with all of that weight.

When he left me alone and I got up, I slipped into some shoes that were at the door and I left the house as quickly as I could. There was a rainstorm that night and I was out in the rain trying to run down the street, weeping, with my huge pregnant belly. My two children were at the front door crying to me, for me to come back. It was a bad storm, raining and thundering. I was running in the rain, down the street, on my way to jump into the Detroit River.

Once again, I felt hopeless, helpless, powerless, in despair, diminished, tormented and defeated. On my way to the river, I got tired. I stopped at a phone booth and called, (collect, because I had no money), my friend Renee, who had also experienced a lot of domestic violence. I told her what happened and what I was getting ready to do.

Renee "talked me off the ledge." I went back home, being calm and quiet, comforted my children and contemplated the plan to leave.

Chapter 9

Another Departure

I left again. And when I did leave, shortly thereafter, my husband told me that he knew where I lived and that he was going to drive by and shoot the house up. After that threat, I kept the blinds closed, the door closed and me and my children played on the floor. I reached out to my friend Renee again and she started talking to me about faith, asking God to help me and having faith that God would help. Renee talked to me on the phone, until about 2 or 3am one time, to no avail. I couldn't grasp "faith" from her conversation. She told me to ask God for faith.

When I got off of the phone with Renee, I did just that. This was the beginning of my conscious "spiritual journey."

Chapter 10

I Still Want My Family

Getting back to my story, when I finally gave birth to our third child, my husband had calmed down and was nice again. He came to the hospital and was very supportive. Now, we were back to trying to be a family again. This time I had my own house. I had been taking karate to protect myself from him, in case the violence started again. I was a brown belt, advancing well, until my car broke down and I had to quit. Then, one day, my husband and I had an argument at my new house. He told me that if I tried that karate sh*t on him he would shoot me. I remember feeling defeated, thinking, "How in the world can I make this family situation work?"

The arguments continued without the violence. The put-downs also continued. But then there were the good times, too, when it seemed that we were moving forward and doing well. It was at those times that I confided in him, talking to him about how I was engaging in some healing work, praying, meditation and listening to positive tapes with subliminal messages on them.

One day, during an argument, he got mad and used my information against me, telling me how my healing practices would not work. And guess what he called me? This man called me a "subliminal motherf*cker."

I laugh now, but I was so hurt then. I cried and told my friends what he called me. They were a good support system. They helped me to focus on the progress that I was making personally and spiritually.

Chapter 11

Enough

Here comes my defining moment. I know you have been hoping and/or waiting for it. That "one day" came, in my own house, where my husband was yelling, and swearing at me. I don't remember what the argument was about, but it was bad. He walked up and got in my face threatening to beat my a**. I stood there, not backing down. I looked him dead in his eyes and told him that he could do whatever he was going to do to me, and if I still had breath in my body after he finished beating me up, then I was going to get off that floor and call the police and find a way to get him prosecuted to the fullest extent of the law!

I was tired of being beaten. I was done. No more. Game over. Enough! And guess what; He left without touching me and I never turned back. I was finally done with that marriage and I eventually divorced him.

Chapter 12

A Blessing in Disguise

Enter my new life of living as a divorced mother, raising my three kids on my own. I was 24 years old, and I just got my new lease on life. I eventually got on welfare (I was the first person in my family to be on welfare) so that I could stay home and raise my infant son and my toddler daughter. My oldest son was about 8 years old then.

I had to figure things out. I had to make things work. I didn't love or value myself, but I did love and value my children.

I focused on them and tried to be the best mother that I could. I felt good about getting away from my ex-husband, as it related to our marital relationship, but I still had to maintain a co-parenting relationship with him. This was often challenging. There were many times when he called the house to talk to the kids and he and I would argue. I got to the point where I would pick up the phone, and if I heard his voice, I would hand it to our kids, telling them that their dad was on the phone, just to avoid conflict.

I had been through enough trauma and drama. I was in need of some serious, productive change in my life. I needed to be uplifted, rather than torn down. I was ready to move forward. I wanted a better life! Well, the change that I needed, came by way of a blessing in disguise.

Remember the threat that I mentioned earlier in my story where my ex-husband told me that he was going to drive by and shoot up the house? As horrifying as it was, that threat was the catalyst to me consciously starting my spiritual journey. That threat led me to God. That night, after I prayed my prayer to God, asking about faith, my life started changing for the better. I would pray, asking God for certain things to occur and they started showing up, left and right.

At first, I thought it was coincidental. Then, I started getting a bit nervous, because it seemed freaky, even surreal. After so many things continued to manifest after I prayed, I got it!

I knew what Faith was. I learned that it is a trust that is developed (for me anyway) over time, a trust where I could ask God for something (guidance, direction, peace, strength or a thing) and know that God would reveal to me or provide for me, in His own time, whatever I prayed for. Hence, I didn't have to worry. I just had to be patient and pay attention to possible signs, messages, or when that thing is delivered.

For instance, after I had left my ex-husband, and was on welfare, I prayed for some school clothes for my son because school was starting soon and I didn't have any money. Did school clothes show up at my front door? No, but several $25 coupons from Montgomery Ward™ did. I didn't even have to spend money to use the coupons. I was so happy and grateful.

I also needed school supplies for my son and I got store coupons advertising that I could get 10 things for $1 (10 pencils for $1, 10 packs of paper for $1, 10 folders or spiral notebooks for $1, etc.). So, to bring the story home, something bad was the catalyst to something good.

A blessing in disguise led to me beginning my conscious relationship with God. And, I must say that having faith in something other than myself, something that is reliable, was and still is a saving grace for me. My relationship with God has led me to have an attitude of gratitude.

Chapter 13

My Church Experience

Now that I had "God on my side," I started to feel more hopeful about life. Things were working much smoother for me. Just knowing that God was with me took some of my stress away. I began to learn that if God did not bring something directly to me, Our Creator would provide guidance on how I should approach a situation so that I could get it myself. Then came church. My best friend, Val, with whom I'd hung out since high school, one day told me that a pastor, along with a group of her congregation came to her house and talked to her about God. They invited her to their church. Val wanted to go, but not alone. So Val asked me to go with her and I did. To make a long story shorter, I liked what I was learning about God and the biblical stories, so I continued to go to church.

Val stopped going because she said that she felt like a hypocrite. You see, on the weekends, Val and I used to smoke weed together and drink Golden Champales. As for me, I continued to smoke, drink and go to church. Val just couldn't do it. Eventually, my smoking and drinking discontinued after I attended the church for a period of time. This was an Apostolic church and smoking and drinking were definitely a "No, No." While attending the church, I had some remarkable experiences.

I received the Holy Spirit, I spoke in tongues, and I also started having visions of the future that came true. I was having all of those experiences, and I hadn't believed in any of that stuff before it happened to me.

Buckle your seatbelt! You are not going to believe one of the visions that I had. One morning, before I went to church, I had a vision of the minister grabbing me by my collar, then I looked into her eyes and saw evil.

Next, after seeing the evil, I knew that it was time to go and find another church. Just prior to that vision, I started questioning her interpretation of the Bible in Sunday school. I was starting to realize that she was off point on some things.

Because my vision had frightened me, that Sunday morning I got my kids dressed more slowly than usual and we were late for church.

We walked in, sat down, and my youngest son, whom I was potty training at the time, had to go to the bathroom. I held up my one finger, stood up, and lowered my head to take him to the bathroom. The minister stopped preaching, looked at me, and told me to sit down. I sat down. My son kept telling me that he had to go to the bathroom. So I went through the same proper etiquette, once again, finger up, stood up, head down to take him to the bathroom. The minister told me to sit down once again. I told her about my son having to go to the bathroom. She said that I should have taken him to the bathroom before I left home. I told her that I did.

Another lady in the church said, "I'll take him." The minister let her take my son to the bathroom. Then, the minister started talking about me while she was preaching. She didn't use my name but everyone knew she was talking about me.

She said, "Y'all want to come in here and do what you want to do, wearing make-up, perming your hair, wearing jewelry, having a whole lot of clothes. I told y'all all you need to do is have two dresses, one at home hanging up to dry and the other one on your back when you are at church. Then you give your extra money to the church, not to the clothing stores."

Side note: I was a fashion designer and I was making new dresses for church all the time. I purchased my fabric from the $1 yard fabric store so it was not expensive for me to make these clothes. Also, I was the only one in church wearing make-up, perming my hair and wearing jewelry.

During Bible school, the minister showed me scripture which she interpreted it to be a sin to wear make-up and jewelry, and to perm hair. I told her, during Bible study, that the scripture she interpreted did not mean the same thing to me and that I would discontinue what I was doing if I saw scripture that did state that these things were a sin. Every now and again, different members of the congregation seemed to agree with various points that I would make during Bible study.

Okay, back to the story: As she was preaching that Sunday morning, it was frustrating for me to sit there listening to her berate me. But, whatever; I sat there and took her jabs. Eventually, the lady who took my son to the bathroom brought my son back. He came and sat next to me and my other two children and the service continued.

Next thing I knew, the pastor started talking about my children, commenting on my son that I was potty training. She made other negative comments, but I don't even remember all of them. Well, I dealt with her talking about me, but I really didn't like her talking about my kids, so I told them to get up, so that we could leave. We stood up and headed toward the back of the church where our coats were hung on the rack next to the entrance to the church.

First, I put on my full-length maxi leather coat (I told you this for a reason). Then, I was getting ready to put the coats on my little ones and realized that the minister was walking down the aisle toward me, talking about me.

She got right in my face and, oh my God! She grabbed me by my collar, just like in my vision, and she said, "God told me that I'm not going to have a lot of people in my church. Get out of my church right now."

I think I had that vision so that when she grabbed me, I wouldn't instantly do my karate moves for that kind of attack, because the minister was an 80-year-old woman and I could have done some real damage.

So, I didn't do any of my moves on her. But I did look into her eyes and I saw that darkness, that evilness, that I saw in my vision. Anyway, while I was looking in her eyes, I said, "Get your hands off of me right now!"

Well, what I didn't see in my vision was a punch from the church lady standing next to me and the pastor. This church lady hit me and said, "Don't you talk to the pastor like that."

Because she was not in my vision, my martial arts instincts kicked in when she hit me, and my fist instantly went between me and the pastor and landed on that lady's face. I punched her in her eye. I think she was wearing glasses. Now, it was on and poppin.

The pastor must have moved back and the congregation moved in and started attacking me. I was leaning against the church pew throwing fists, swinging at whoever was attacking me. My oldest son was about 10 years old and he was a brown belt in karate like me, so of course, he started helping me fight. That's right, me and my 10-year-old son, fighting all these church people who were now physically attacking both of us.

What happened next? The pastor's son, who was about 6' 5" and slim, grabbed me from the back, in a full nelson. He had me at least one and a half feet off the floor. Well, I know what moves to do in a full nelson, so I tried them, but my feet kept getting hung up in my full-length maxi leather coat, so I couldn't land one of my kicks. No matter how hard I tried to wiggle in the air to get around my own coat, my feet kept getting caught in it.

Shaking my head, I realized this was a mess. Then, the next thing I knew, this guy had taken me outside and he threw me down on the sidewalk. He threw me so hard that my high heel shoe went four lanes over, into the street. I got up. I was stunned!

Then, I saw my oldest son outside with me. *But where were my little ones? Oh no, they were still in the church!* I started banging on the church doors, yelling, "Give me my kids, give me my kids." They finally pushed my kids out the door. Then I realized that my kids' coats were still inside of the church. So I once again banged on the church doors, this time yelling, "Give me my kids' coats!" They opened the church doors just a little and slid my kids' coats through the door. I put my little ones' coats on and tried to compose myself. Then, I heard music in the church. It started getting louder and louder. You will never guess what song they started singing. I couldn't believe it either. They were singing, *We are Fighting for Jesus*!

Damn. What a day!

Chapter 14

Let's Try Church Again

After that church debacle, I was on a quest for a new church home. I visited churches, without my kids, of course. I needed for them to be safe. When I finally found a church, my oldest son would not go. Could you blame him? My son had not only witnessed his dad fighting me, he also witnessed the church congregation, at least 20 adults, fighting me. Bless his heart, he jumped in to help.

The new church home that I found was wonderful. It's worship used to come on television every Sunday and I watched it. I was checking out the minister and looking at the congregation, who all appeared pleasant. The church focused on love and all kinds of positive messages, unlike the church wherein I was assaulted.

The church was called Church of Today. It was a Unity Church. Then, the name was changed to Renaissance Unity. We started going to church regularly. This place was awesome. My younger two children loved going to this church, as did I. Great teachers used to come there to speak, such as Dr. Wayne Dyer, Dr. Deepak Chopra, Les Brown, Shakti Gawain and more. Marianne Williamson eventually became our minister.

I grew spiritually, mentally and emotionally as a result of attending that church. I also grew from reading the books in the church's fabulous bookstore. I attended a lot of the church's workshops and seminars. In addition, I learned a great deal from my spiritual teacher at that time, Carolyne, aka, "Isis."

As a result of everything that I have learned, mentally, emotionally, and spiritually, I am in a phenomenal space in my life and I'm still growing. Maybe some of you have sought faith and a church home, so you'll understand the importance of this aspect of my journey.

Chapter 15

My Brain Rewiring

In the late 80's, I started the process of rewiring my brain. Back then, I, as well as others in the spiritual circles in which I traveled, deemed the changes to be of a spiritual nature. The changes were taking place in ways that seemed mysterious. I went to workshops to learn how to do "image pages," now called "vision boards." I started creating pages and focusing on them and the things that I focused on seemed to just show up in my life.

Sometimes, I was mysteriously guided to things that I had put on my pages. I practiced visualization, as well.

My life started changing as my focus and belief systems started changing. I learned how to consciously create dynamics in my life. I started using affirmations to rewire my thinking process, my beliefs about what I could accomplish, and what I intended to manifest.

I recorded my affirmations, saying them slowly with meditation music playing in the background. I listened to my affirmation's recordings at least two times a day. I looked at my vision boards throughout the day, as they were on my walls and I saw them when I passed by. I created mantras and I said them, as needed. I consciously worked on focusing on productive thoughts, rather than stinkin' thinkin'.

I also practiced meditation every morning. Meditation increased my experience of my inner world, as I shut out the outside world to meditate. Going inward in my meditations led me to practice what is now called "Quantum Jumping," whereby I got in touch with my Higher Self and allowed her to guide me to the point where I merged with that part of my Self.

I went from not loving and valuing myself to loving, valuing, appreciating, and enjoying myself. I've gone from being on welfare to being a PsyD with four college degrees to my name. I'm a business owner. I own my private practice. I have traveled around the world and studied in other countries. I've got stamps on every page of my last passport and now I have a new one to work on.

I live by the water in a place that I love. I have a boat that I love. I have timeshares in other countries. Also, I have a wardrobe that I love. I have a host of positive people in my life. I am living my dream that I consciously created from the vision boards, visualizations and affirmations that I used to assist with rewiring my brain.

I have been to a mental and emotional kind of hell and back and I was still able to rewire my brain and create a life that I enjoy. I really want you to know that you can rewire your brain, as well. No matter what your backstory contains, you can change. If you have a history of trauma, you will have to work a little more than the average person, but you can do it. My backstory is riddled with trauma and drama and I rewired my brain.

Choose you. Choose happiness. Choose life designed by you, rather than operating from someone else's program for your life. Start today. *Rewire your brain!*

PART 2
THE JOURNEY OF CHANGE

TIME TO GET IN THE DRIVER'S SEAT

I've come to know that our bodies are our vehicles. We exist in them. We are energetic streams of consciousness, spirits, existing in a body/vehicle. Our vehicles come fully-equipped with a brain that mostly operates on automatic pilot, on unconscious programs. "Unconscious" doesn't mean you're asleep, it just means you aren't aware of what your brain is doing most of the time. You aren't aware of what your phone does when you're not using it; you just know that it's working like it's programmed. You depend on that, just like you depend on your brain.

It is important to know that some of the programs in our brain are taking us places we don't even want to go. Once we learn how to rewire our brains, and consciously create our own programs, this puts us in the driver's seat of our vehicle. Once you are in the driver's seat of your vehicle, buckle your seatbelt, because you have opened up a whole new realm of possibilities that puts you on the roadmap to living your dreams.

Introduction

I invite you to participate in an exciting journey of self-discovery, wherein you will experience a new level of empowerment and freedom. As you come into the knowledge and wisdom that you will gain as a result of employing the tools and strategies in this part of the book, you will come to know the power that you have to redefine and recreate yourself!

In the next section of this book, you are going to learn how to rewire your brain. Neuroplasticity is what will allow you to do it. While the next section includes information about neuroplasticity and other concepts that I present in this introduction, I believe that the information is important and worth repeating, as it can help you to gain a greater understanding into what you will read, moving forward. Neuroplasticity is the new term on the scene for rewiring your brain. To make it simple, neuroscientists/brain scientists have recently discovered things about the brain that they had not known. With the introduction of new technologies, the scientists no longer just explore what goes wrong with the brain, in cases like Parkinson's or Alzheimer's, for example, neuroscientists have been looking at "normal" brains to see how they work, as it relates to habits.

For decades, people have often spoken about how we are wired to do certain things, and now, science has discovered more about that wiring process. You might wonder why all of this is important. Well, let me tell you the significance of this grand discovery. Neuroscientists discovered that within the brain, there are neurons/nerves that fire together then wire together. In other words, when neurons/nerves in the brain communicate with each other by delivering electrical and chemical signals, in a repetitious manner, this causes the neurons/nerves in the brain to form connections. Those connections are home to our habits. Yes, our habits reside in structures of the brain, which are called neural networks. And, these neural networks determine our habits; hence, our habitual way of thinking about certain things and of course our habitual behavioral responses to things.

Now that scientists know how our brains get wired, they now know how we can rewire our brain. You rewire it the same way that you wired it in the first place; by doing the same thing over and over again. Yeppers, it's just that simple. If you keep thinking the same way over and over again about certain topics, your neurons will start firing that way and the more the same neurons continue to fire together, they wire together and create a habit. It's kind of like the way we make friends.

If you keep communicating with the same person over and over again, you start to experience a connection with them. Eventually, as you continue to communicate with that same person over and over again, like a significant other, for instance, you get used to being around them because you now have a habit of interacting with that person. At some time in your life if you and that person break off the relationship, it is usually difficult to move on, even if you know that person was not good for you. Why? Because the habit/neural network in your brain still continues to fire in the same ways because those neurons are wired together. Even if you stay away from that person, you will still have thoughts of them because your relationship with them is wired into your brain. Eventually and hopefully, you do move on if that person is not good for you. How do you move on? You move on by thinking and doing things differently, over and over and over and over again! Have you ever heard the expression, getting a person "out of your system?" It's something to be said about that.

Getting a person out of your system means that you have actually changed your habit of how you thought about them and how you interacted with them. You caused different nerves/neurons in your brain to start firing together until they eventually wired together and put you on a different habitual path. I say habitual path because, drum roll please.........., according to neuroscience, the brain is wired for habits, with 95% of our thoughts and behaviors being unconscious brain activity (habits) and only a whopping 5% being conscious thought. Isn't that something; only 5% of how we think and what we do is actually conscious thought and 95% is unconscious (habitual) brain activity, which includes thoughts and behaviors (*certain bodily functions are also part of unconscious brain activity). This means that most of the time, we are walking around on automatic pilot (habits).

There is actually a school of thought around why this is so. A quick back story: We have the same brain as the early humans who walked the planet with saber tooth tigers, and, in order for the human species to endure such a menacing threat, the human brain set itself up for survival. Way, way back in the day when humans were in the wilderness and heard or saw a saber tooth tiger, their stress response for fight or flight would kick in. Because the tiger could mean the end of life, humans either had to fight the tigers or go into flight mode and run like crazy. With that in mind, it is important to know that when the human brain engages in conscious thought, that process uses a lot of energy. When the human brain engages in unconscious thought (habits), there is not a lot of energy that is expended. If the early humans had spent most of their waking life thinking consciously, they would not have enough energy to fight or get away in flight mode from the saber tooth tigers, and all humans would have ceased to exist. You and I would have never made it to the planet.

So, the brain, for survival's sake, was wired to operate on 95% habitual unconscious brain activity, which includes thoughts and behaviors, and 5% conscious thought to conserve energy. To help you connect this concept to your own life, I will provide this example; You have more than likely experienced how draining it is to engage in conscious thinking, especially if you have ever had to do a lot of learning in a day's time, for example as a high school or college student or either in regard to something pertaining to your work-life.

After studying or focusing on material for a significant part of your day, near the end of the day it might be difficult to recall all of the information that you know you just studied. You try to recall it but end up with the frustrating process of your brain buffering for a period of time and then shutting down, no matter how many times you restart this process. What has likely happened is that you have literally used up most of your brain's energy so it can no longer process all of your thoughts. You have to get some rest and try again at a later time. It's like we have so many energy bits that we can use in a day for processing information and making decisions, and after those bits are used up, we are left with low functioning brain power.

Ironically, the new neuroplasticity findings remind me of some age-old knowledge. As I studied the scientific information, I couldn't help but think about certain scriptures in the Bible; Be ye transformed by the renewing of your mind, *"As a man thinketh so is he."* Interesting connection; you can rewire your brain by thinking and doing things in a different way and hence change/transform your life.

Accordingly, as the Bible states, *"Be ye transformed (changed) by the renewing of your mind."* (Rewiring your brain?); consistent concept. As a man thinketh, so is he; Keep thinking the same way, "so is you", nothing is going to change in your life, other than some of the people with whom you interact? As a matter of fact, the dynamics in your life (your issues and challenges) will remain basically the same, as well, because you have not changed your thinking and if you have not changed your thinking, your behaviors won't change.

Here is another golden nugget of old knowledge; Insanity is doing the same thing over and over expecting different results. Keep doing what you are doing and you will keep getting what you are getting in life. And as previously noted, keep thinking how you are thinking and you will keep getting what you are getting, as well. I will even take this a step further and state that if you don't change for the better, some of the dynamics in your life will be made worse by the new people in your life, because they will basically think and act like you as well as those same other people who were previously in your life. You draw these types of people into your life because birds of a feather flock together. Hence, you draw people in your life because in some way they match you, perhaps via your belief systems, ways of thinking or your behaviors.

Now, I want you to be prepared for this; if you change your way of thinking and behaving in the direction of what is best for you, eventually, you will no longer experience the same connection with the people in your life who matched you when you were on a negative or destructive path. Once you realize the change or perhaps an awkwardness in these relationships, it will be better for you to "get them out of your system."

However, because we all have free will, if you like or you are ok with what you are getting from life then keep doing what you are doing and thinking what you are thinking. If you don't like what is showing up in your life, and you want things to change, then you have to start thinking and doing things differently. This means that you will have to take a more active position in your life. This means that you have to identify what you want to experience in your life. If you can't identify the specifics, that's ok, you can start with generalities, for example, being happy or having peace of mind. Whatever you do, it would be most beneficial for you to identify something because like that old saying goes, if you don't know what you stand for you might fall for anything!

Side Note: The Spirit of These Times
Sometimes we change because we want to experience something better. Sometimes we change because life's conditions warrant change. Throughout the course of history, one thing is for certain, people have always experienced change! When the pendulum swings, we find ourselves in positions that may be favorable or unfavorable. Nevertheless, we have always found a way to rise above. We've all heard stories from our elders about how things were different in their day and they had to adapt to various situations (change).

In our past, in just growing up from the time we were babies to getting to where we are now, we have been impacted by a number of circumstances and life transitions, which led to us adopting a new way of being in the world (change). Again, today, as we are faced with the spirit of these times, wherein much change is occurring worldwide, it is imperative that we consciously identify our place and decide where and how our next journey of change begins.

As you likely know, globally, our human species is experiencing a tremendous gravity of change. This change has impacted people's health, family-life, work-life, social-life, education, and financial and living situations. Further, people are experiencing grief due to the loss of loved ones, and more and more people are being diagnosed with mental health and substance abuse issues. There is no clear-cut timeline in sight, as to when all of these stressful events will come to an end. As information continues to unfold, it appears to me, that we are moving toward a whole new level of change that has been called "a new normal"!

What will your "new normal" look like? Before you attempt to answer that, remember, that we can influence the direction that our "new normal" (habits) will take. How can we do that; by rewiring our brain! We can start putting our time and energy into rewiring our brain and consciously making choices that are in alignment with what we choose for ourselves. It is important to choose for ourselves because if you don't work to consciously create your own new ways of thinking and being in the world (rewiring your brain), then someone else will do that for you. Perhaps that someone is a friend, family member or co-worker. Perhaps that influence will come from what you watch on your television, tablet or cell phone. Yes, our thoughts and behaviors can be influenced by our favorite programs ("programming") on TV, as well as from the various news and social media platforms to which we give our attention.

Nevertheless, wherever the influence comes from, do your due diligence to become as informed as you can about the events that are contributing to the unfolding "new normal" so that you can do what is best for you. Keep in mind that it is best to use discernment in your search for knowledge. If you are feeling a lot of fear, pressure or shame from the sources of information that you are utilizing, you should consider finding platforms that can provide the important information that you need, while leaving you with a sense of hope. Even though there are certain things that are happening that are beyond our control, there are still some things that are within our control (even if it doesn't seem like it). Work to find a sense of balance in your life and maintain it, as you move forward with your "new normal"

***P.S. This next part of the book is not meant to be read and cannot be read as fast as my backstory. Take your time and mindfully read this section. Take it in and immediately put into practice the tools and strategies that you learn. Be prepared for situations to arise that will allow you to implement these strategies. Remember my back story and your back story along the way. And know that rewiring your brain can and will not happen overnight. Enjoy the journey.

Chapter 16

Your Journey Begins

Are you tired of suffering, tired of feeling upset? Are you tired of life not going the way you want? Are you tired of going through the same things over and over again? Do you want to feel peace, be happy, not be overburdened with stress, depression, and anxiety? Would you like to feel more relaxed and in the flow of life? Would you like to feel more in control of your life, but you just don't know what to do to create positive change?

If you answered yes to any of these questions, you are not alone. Most people, be it your family, friends, neighbors, co-workers, and people you don't even know, feel that they are not living the life they want. A lot of people believe that there is someone else or some "powers-that-be" who have some kind of hold on their lives keeping them from doing the things that they want to do or maybe even becoming who they want to become.

I am here to say that no one has the kind of control over you that you think they have. Heck, most people don't even have control of themselves. People can influence you and try to make you do what they want, but at the end of the day, you have the power of choice. You can choose to say no, you can choose to do and say things that are going to take your life in the direction that you want to go.

As a matter of fact, you have been choosing things throughout your life. Some of your choices were conscious choices, meaning you were aware of what you were choosing. Some of your choices were unconscious choices, meaning that you were not aware of what you were choosing. Say what! Unconscious choosing? Yes, and let me explain how.

Chapter 17

Unconscious Choices and Habits

Did you know that our human brain activity operates 95% from unconscious programs and has 5% available for conscious thought? I won't go too scientific here, instead, I will offer a brief explanation. The human brain is wired for 95% unconscious activity and 5% conscious thought to conserve energy. Just thinking about something uses a lot of our body's energy. For instance, students have to consciously focus on school work and after a while, the brain does not process information with the same speed and accuracy as it did during the previous hours of studying or doing school-work. And, for certain careers, the work consists of constantly figuring things out (conscious thought), and as the day goes on, mental fatigue sets in. Hence, constantly focusing, studying, figuring things out (conscious thought), can be extremely draining. Why is it draining? It is draining because conscious thinking uses up a lot of our energy.

Now, let's go back to the time when humans walked the planet with saber tooth tigers. Oh, let me mention this: We have the same brain as those humans did, however, we have additional structures that developed over time as we evolved. When the humans back then came across the saber tooth tiger, the stress response kicked in (fight/flight), and they needed to have the energy in their bodies to either fight the tiger, possibly hitting it between the eyes with a large stone, or they needed the energy to flee (i.e., get out of Dodge; "bounce" quickly; run… you get the point)! If they did not have the energy to successfully fight or flee, you and I would not exist today. We are here because they survived. I'm sure, that in the beginning stages, a lot of them died off. Overtime, eventually, the brain and the body adapted in a way that they would work together so that humankind could continue their journey on the planet.

The brain wired itself to conserve energy, to have sufficient energy available for the fight/flight response by making us humans' creatures of habit. A habit is an unconscious way of being. We have habitual ways of thinking and habitual ways of behaving which occur 95% of the time. The other 5% is left for more energy-draining conscious thought. Hence, 95% of the time our choices are habits, and again, our habits are unconscious thoughts and behaviors that, for the most part, we are not aware of.

Chapter 18

How We Develop Habits

Simply put, we have cells in our brains called neurons/nerve cells. They communicate with each other so that we humans can function. The neurons communicate via electrical impulses that fire, one to the other. When we do certain things, think or say certain things, specific neurons fire, communicating with each other based on whatever we are doing, thinking or saying. For example, if you keep doing the same thing, the same neuron/nerve cells will fire together. Nerves that fire together, wire together and that's what creates your habits.

Our brain is full of cells that have wired together. They are called neural networks (habits, habits and more habits). Hence, if you keep doing something over and over again, thinking in a certain way over and over again, then you develop habits, habitual ways of behaving and thinking.

This means that your brain is programmed to operate on automatic pilot, repetitiously doing, and thinking in certain ways whether you like it or not. These habits occur without us having to think about them. They just happen. They get triggered/activated, and it's on a popping! Habits are unconscious; 95% of your brain is wired for unconscious activity.

Chapter 19

You Can Change: Rewire Your Brain

Hold up, you are not off the hook. Even though your brain is wired for 95% unconscious activity, that doesn't mean you are not responsible for your bad, unproductive habits. Are you that person or do you know somebody who says "That's just the way I am," or "He's just wired that way." Regardless of however you are wired, if you are not getting what you want in life, it is in your best interests to change. How do you change? I'm glad you asked. It's about Neuroplasticity; the brain's ability to rewire itself.

Yes, you can change the wiring in your brain.
You can interrupt current brain activity patterns and build new brain patterns (i.e., build/create new habits). You change your current patterns/habits in the same way that you created them, by doing or thinking about something over and over again. However, in order to change your current habits, you have to be conscious, be aware, pay attention to what you are saying and doing. You've got to be Johnny-on-the-spot (not 100% of the time). When that unproductive

habit pops up, you have to notice it and then consciously make yourself do the new identified behavior or switch to the new way of thinking.

I almost forgot to mention that you have to identify what habits you want to change and identify what new habits you want in their place. Then, when the bad habit rears its ugly head, *BAM*, you catch it quickly and do your thing.

What is your thing? Like I said, your thing is consciously making yourself do, say or think, in other words, implement the new desired behavior/habit the moment that you become aware of an undesired habit being triggered. Simply, when your current unwanted habit is triggered, make yourself engage in your new, desirable behavior or way of thinking. Once you do your new thing over and over and over again, you will create your new habit.

Remember, nerves that fire together wire together. So, get started! It's time to download some new and improved programs into your computer/brain. Rewire your brain.

Chapter 20

Programs as Belief Systems

Programs, yes, that's right, you have programs in your brain. Your programming consists of all of your habits, including your belief systems, that are programmed to activate when they get triggered.

Triggers, wow that's another topic to be discussed a little later. Let's address programs.

Do you know some of your programming? Do you know how you got some of your programming? If you are old school, you might remember this program about money, "money don't grow on trees," and "you gotta rob Peter to pay Paul." Hearing this kind of programming formulates a belief system about the scarcity of money (i.e., you don't have enough money to do the things you need to do or want to do). That programming came from back in the day when parents had financial struggles.

While the struggle was real, they taught/programmed their kids to believe that there will never be enough money for whatever the purpose may be. While most people in the United States live from paycheck to paycheck, we do now have more millionaires than we ever had in history. Maybe they didn't get that message, or maybe they did but found a way to change their programming.

A program that a lot of people struggle with today is the program of not being good enough. I've talked to a lot of people in my practice with this download. Some people get this programing from people in their life who put them down, or maybe they just don't fit in, and this makes them feel that they are "not good enough." Others can never do enough in someone's eyes, and end up feeling like they are "not good enough." There are also "not good enough" downloads that come from the media, advertising, and the like that send a message like this: If you want to be cool, beautiful, successful, then you have to look a certain way (that doesn't look like you), or have certain things that you really can't afford (but might get them anyway during a retail therapy trip).

Social media is packed with all kinds of things that can send the message that you are "not good enough." Unfortunately, sometimes even tragically, a lot of teenagers buy into this, hook, line and sinker.

It is important to note that not all programs are negative or unhealthy. You do have some positive, productive, healthy habits/programs. It's your job to determine what programs are working for your highest good and which ones are not. I say, weed out the ones that are not working for you.

I like the quote by Harley Davidson: "When writing the story of your life, never let anyone else hold the pen."

So pick up your pen and start writing. Identify what habits/programs you need to have in your life and make the necessary changes so that you can live the life of your choosing. Take charge of your life. Rewire your brain.

Chapter 21

Triggers

Situational Triggers

Triggers are your hot buttons, those things in life that activate, that fire up, your habits. A trigger can be as simple as when you see this, you do that; when you hear this, you think it means that; when you get involved in this, you act like that; or when someone does this, you think it always means that. In short, situations trigger or activate a specific habit, whether it is a habitual behavior, or a habitual way of perceiving something.

Oftentimes, triggers are things we cannot control. For example, a trigger could be something that someone else is doing. A trigger could be something someone else says. A trigger could be a rule, a law, a situation. Nevertheless, no matter what the trigger, if you stop and think (be conscious and aware) before you go on autopilot and unconsciously act out your habit, you have a better chance of taking your life where you want it to go.

Many people claim the victim role when they get triggered. They go on automatic pilot, proclaiming that the negative outcome would have never happened if that other person had not said or done whatever they said or did.

Remember we have the power to choose. You have the ability to respond to situations in a conscious manner, in a thoughtful, aware manner. You can enhance your ability to respond to situations in a more responsible way by practicing a simple strategy: *Stop and think, before you act.*

By doing this, you are not stopping the trigger that activates your habit, you are putting yourself in a position to make a conscious choice, rather than acting from an unconscious space (habit).

If you deem the habitual response to be for your highest good, go for it, but if it's not, don't create another setback for yourself by doing or saying something, or focusing on thoughts that are not going to take you where you want to go in life.

Get more of what you want out of life. Become aware of your triggers. *Stop and think before you act.* Do away with the bad habits and download the new ones. Rewire your brain.

Thoughts as Triggers

Have you ever gotten triggered by your own thoughts? A situation could have happened last week and you've been sitting around stewing on it, focusing on stinkin' thinkin', making up all kinds of scenarios in your head, and getting more and more distressed about it.

You get yourself so worked up that you end up taking action. Maybe it's shooting someone a heated ALL CAPS text or email. Maybe it's making a phone call to give someone "a piece of your mind." Maybe you call someone else to vent, gossip and get them worked up too. Maybe you break up with your significant other, only to take them back after realizing you didn't have all your facts straight.

Here is a very important tip about thoughts: All the thoughts that pop into your head are not true. That's right. Just because a thought pops in does not mean it is based on reality. A thought is just a thought. It is important to practice discernment with your thoughts. Ask yourself, *is this thought true? How do I know that this thought is 100% true?*

Thoughts can get creative in your head, putting together a movie in your brain that has nothing to do with the truth, and you will be all messed up about it. Your emotions will be real, with an uppercase "R," while the thoughts that led to those emotions were some real untrue, inaccurate thoughts. Well, what are we supposed to do with this information? After all, many of us are taught that we are supposed to value our thoughts and feelings.

Great question and I'm glad you asked, or maybe you were thinking along those lines. I would say, value yourself and acknowledge what you are feeling. Then, ask yourself why you are feeling that way if you are distressed. If you get quiet and pay attention to your thoughts, you will be able to tune in to the scenario or movie playing out in your brain, that led to your distress.

Once you are tuned in, ask yourself, *Is this true?* If it is not true, then tell yourself that the creative story or movie is not true. Maybe you need more information to fill in some blanks. Rather than allowing yourself to focus on the untrue thoughts, because they will keep popping in, do something to distract yourself so you can focus on something positive, uplifting or productive.

Don't focus on those untrue thoughts anymore. When they pop in, say a mantra, which is a short statement that makes you feel ok, good, positive, or productive.
The importance of saying the mantra is that you are now focusing on a productive thought which will, in turn, lead you to have a desirable feeling. If you have a habit of focusing on stinkin' thinkin', stop it!

You can't control what thoughts pop into your head, but you can control what you do with them. You can choose to focus on the thoughts or make a conscious choice to not focus on the thoughts. You can make a choice to focus on a mantra, or distract yourself by focusing on something positive, such as videos of funny or cute babies or puppies, or outrageous acts on singing or dancing competition shows.

Take action now. Consciously choose what to focus on. Rewire your brain.

Chapter 22

Thought/Feeling Connection

I want to make sure that you get the concept of the thought/feeling connection. It is worth mentioning again. When you focus on thoughts, whether you are conscious of focusing on them or not, you will get a feeling based upon the nature of those thoughts. If the thought is negative or destructive, the emotions you will experience will be distressing and you may feel anxiety, anger, fear, shame, guilt, or other uncomfortable emotions.

If you focus on a thought that is productive or positive, you will experience pleasurable emotions like happiness, calmness, peacefulness, and tranquility. You will be able to tell what kinds of thoughts you're focusing on by paying attention to how you feel. It is important to note that some situations do not lend themselves to a positive perspective, however, you can look at that situation from a productive or healthy perspective.

It is also important to note that sometimes your thoughts can really "fly below the radar" of your awareness, where you are not even aware that you are focusing on them. Nevertheless, how you feel is still a telltale sign that you are focusing on stinkin' thinkin'.

To illustrate that, I have a funny story. About 20 years ago, during a relationship issue, I was very upset about something that happened. I do like to process things so that I can learn any lessons that might be presented within my challenges, however, that one day, my brain went beyond processing.

My brain went to the left, with all kinds of negative thoughts popping in. I was working my program by continuously saying my mantra. Then, I decided that I needed a distraction, a movie to focus on. So, I turned on the TV to find a movie. I couldn't really find anything that I wanted to watch, so I selected a movie that I had seen before, many, many times. Yes, I really liked that movie at the time. Here comes the funny part! After sitting in the chair "watching the movie" for about 30 minutes, staring directly at the TV, I realized that the movie version was in Spanish, without subtitles.

I don't even know Spanish, I don't speak Spanish, other than a few numbers! I started laughing so hard, because I realized that while I was staring at the TV, I was focusing on stinkin' thinkin' rather than the movie. Since my brain knew what was going to happen next in the movie, it was not focusing on what the characters were saying. My stinkin' thinkin' was below the radar of my conscious awareness, while I was staring at the TV. That situation was so funny to me that it stole the show from the stinkin' thinkin' scenarios.

So, if you find yourself deep down in the stinkin' thinkin' while you are trying to work your program, don't sweat it. Laugh at yourself and keep it moving. I did.

Keep practicing. Rewire your brain.

Chapter 23

Reticular Activating System

There is a structure in our brain called the Reticular Activating System (RAS). This structure works behind the scenes, revealing to you things that are relevant to you in your "mini universe." You have experienced it in action before, but likely did not know what was going on.

For instance, you are in the market for a vehicle. As you explore your options, you hone in on the vehicle that you want. Then, all of a sudden, you start seeing that vehicle everywhere. Or you might make your purchase first and then start seeing your vehicle everywhere. Now we know that you didn't all of a sudden get beamed up into a parallel universe where a lot of people are driving the same model vehicle as yours.

So what is really going on? What happened is, when you made up your mind about what vehicle you wanted, that particular vehicle became relevant to you. As a result, your

RAS allowed you to be able to see what was already present in the world around you.

You might be thinking: *What do you mean, that it allowed me to see what is already here? There is nothing wrong with my eyes, my glasses or my contacts.*

Once again, I'm glad you asked. I'll make it simple, so as to get to the point. There are so many things present in the world around us. It would be overwhelming to the brain to process everything that is out there. It's like this: Our brain can only process a certain amount of data per second and a certain amount of information in a day.

Our subconscious brain, where our habits reside, can process something like 11 million bits of data per second. And our brain's prefrontal cortex, which controls conscious thinking, cannot even process one million bits of data per second from the environment.

Let's say we need to have the ability to process sextillion (that's a real number with 21 zeros), bits of data per second to process everything in the world around us, but we just don't have that kind of brainpower. So the job of the RAS is to allow you to be aware of things relevant to you, like your habits, belief systems, things you focus on, and things that you have been taught, so that you won't deplete your brainpower by perceiving things that are not relevant to you.

The human brain does not have enough power to process everything around us, so the RAS basically keeps our brain in line so that we don't blow a fuse or start buffering and become mentally and physically wiped out by mid-day. It also keeps us from being disoriented and from seeing or sensing things that we do not understand. So, when you add something new to your list of things to do, your RAS will allow you to see that new thing, as in the example of the vehicle preference or purchase. That vehicle did not become relevant to you until you decided that you wanted it. Now that it is relevant, your RAS allows you to see it.

I know I said that I was going to keep it simple, but I want to take you on a brief *Journey Down The Rabbit Hole.* So here we go. According to quantum physics, everything is energy vibrating at a certain frequency. Everything is connected to everything else through various fields. This means that while things appear to be one way, for example, if you observe them through a high-powered microscope or some other ocular technology, you will observe something different. You see, our senses actually interpret vibration, and send messages to our brain. Our eyes interpret vibration, and we see. Our ears interpret vibration and we hear. Did you know that there is no such thing, really, as color?

When we see what we call color, what is happening is that light energy for each "color" is vibrating at a different frequency and each of the different frequencies appears to us as different "colors." Also, there are some "colors" that our eyes cannot see such as ultraviolet and infrared, because the naked eye is not able to interpret those vibrations. There is a large spectrum of "color" and the human eye alone, without technology, can only interpret a limited amount of vibrations in the "color" spectrum.

Also, do you remember that age-old question that asks, "If a tree falls in the rainforest and no one was there to hear it, does it make a sound?" Well, the answer is "no." Why is that? Because sound is what we experience when our ears interpret vibrations.

So if there was no one around with ears to interpret the vibration of the tree falling as sound, then sound did not occur. The only thing that occurred was that energy moved when the tree fell. So let's crawl out of the rabbit hole for now and come back into our holographic universe. Oops sorry, still in the rabbit hole.

Okay, now we are out of the rabbit hole for sure, seriously! With the notion from my brief explanation of energy and frequencies, think about how much stuff is in our world or around you wherever you are in this moment. There is just too much going on for us to interpret.

Here is a question for you: Would you want to interpret everything around you?

Before you answer that question, check this out: You do know that just as we live on planet earth, we humans are host to all kinds of microorganisms inside of our bodies, on our skin, eyelashes, hair, and so on. Do you want to see all of that stuff walking, slithering, crawling on you? Probably not. Is it relevant for us to see all of that? Probably not. Is it relevant for all of those microorganisms to be aware of each other? Yes, because that is the microscopic world that they live in, where they have to survive and do whatever else they do.

To my point, there is too much going on for us to interpret and in this case of microorganisms slithering about on you and in you, my guess is that you don't even want to interpret everything in our universe.

Chapter 24

Strategize to Rewire Your Brain

Once you get into the work of rewiring your brain, you will be identifying good habits that you want to keep and bad, unproductive habits that you want to deactivate and replace with the new good, productive habits.

Write down the new habits that you want to develop. When you write them down, it's like giving your RAS a command to show you a multitude of opportunities where you can employ your strategies to develop your new desired habits.

Allow me to provide an explanation of how our RAS can assist us with changing our habits. Here we go. It's important to know that our habits are basically us, as energy beings moving through sequences of "now moments." Think about having your camera on photo bursts, where it takes a lot of pictures with just one hit of the button. If you are moving, each pic will be a depiction of you in a sequence of different moments, hence, different "now moments." Your RAS will be in tune with all of your "now moments." It will reveal things to you that you said you want to change, and it will reveal those opportunities that can help with that change, at just the *right* "now moments."

The RAS will do this because you have made developing a new habit relevant. Hence, the RAS reveals to us what is relevant to us. So write down the new habits that you want to develop and look at your list a couple times a day. Take a picture of your list on your cell phone so that you will always have it. Start paying more attention to how you move through life. Watch your RAS do its thing. Rewire your brain.

I just talked about identifying habits that you want to change and identifying the new habits that you want to replace them. This strategy is key because you have to know where you are and where you want to go, or else you will be floating in the wind, drifting here and there without direction. Not having direction is like taking a joy ride, letting your current programs drive you through life. Depending on your programs, this ride can take you deep down in the trenches, have you spinning your wheels, getting stuck in the mud, or always climbing what seems like hopeless uphill battles. You will hopefully learn some things, but joy riding will not effectively produce the kind of positive changes that will make your life the best that it can be.

If you want a better life, you have got to get in the driver's seat. When you are in the driver's seat, you can consciously advance your vehicle through life with direction, and purposefully create a life full of positive change. Joy ride or driver's seat, it's your choice.

I prefer the driver's seat and I like having direction. This is why I choose to focus on strategies to consciously create in my life those experiences that I desire. So if you want positive and fulfilling changes in your life sooner than later, take the approach of having direction. Strategize. Know where you want to go, what habits you want to have, and write them down. And remember, your RAS will help you rewire your brain.

Chapter 25

Affirmations

Using affirmations is a great way to rewire your brain. You can find all kinds of affirmations on the internet. Identify 10 affirmations that speak to your soul. Write them down. Take a pic of them with your cell phone. Read your affirmations at least twice a day. You can also record yourself saying them with the music of your choice in the background, or soundscapes, tones, or maybe you prefer silence in the background.

Be creative and do what makes your heart sing. Whether you write your affirmations down or record them, repetition is very important. You have to expose yourself to your affirmations regularly. The more you expose yourself to your affirmations, the faster you will rewire your brain. Your affirmations will eventually become your new belief systems. Belief systems occur with exposure to certain thoughts over and over again. Belief systems are a habitual way of thinking.

Remember, rewiring your brain is all about changing habits since the brain operates 95% out of habit, or unconscious brain activity, and 5% conscious thought. Since the brain automatically wires in habits, you might as well have habits wired in that will take you where you want to go in life. Get started with your affirmations. Rewire your brain.

Chapter 26

Vision Boards

Back in the day, we called them "image pages," but now the new catchphrase is "vision board." Regardless, they are the same thing and they work! I've been making these boards and consciously creating positive change in my life for over thirty years. By using vision boards, in addition to affirmations, I have consciously created my life and I am living my dream, at least the dreams that I have had in the past, while I'm now in the midst of creating new dreams to come true.

The way that I like to make vision boards is to go through magazines, brochures, sales papers, and other resources and find and cut out pictures, words, and images that reflect what I want to create or experience in my life. I like to use one board or page for one concept. For example, you can have a health page, family page, financial page, relationship page, or career page, or whatever categories you need.

The creation phase of vision boards is significant. You should pick a space and time when you will not be interrupted so that you can get deeply in touch with your inner guidance system, which you'll see later, and be drawn to the perfect words, pictures and images that will be most productive for you and what you want to create.

It *does not* matter how others might feel about the images; this board is for you and what resonates with your soul. Important, Important, Important: Only select words, pictures, and images that are what you want to experience, not what you want to get away from. For example, on your financial page, do not put the word "broke" on your board, such as, "No more being broke." You don't want the word "broke" swimming around in your consciousness. Instead, use pictures and words that are what you want your brain to focus on, such as "financial prosperity," or "wealth." I think you get the picture.

And if your goal is to be at a weight that is healthier for you than your current weight, don't put "lose the fat" on your vision board. You do not want the word "fat" to be a focus in your consciousness. Instead, use words and images that reflect being healthy, more fit, or slimmer.

After you select and cut out the items for your page or pages, start arranging them on your paper or whatever you are using. I once used a canvas because I could not find the paper that I liked to use. Now, I love the canvas approach, especially because it hangs so nicely on the wall.

Funny story, I used to glue everything on my paper once I got it arranged the way I liked. Let me tell you, the gluing process is no joke. It can take an hour or more, depending on how many items are going on your page. Getting to the funny part, one day my daughter and I made vision boards together. I'm very detailed and I like completion, so I took my time and glued all of my items on my page and it was done. Yes, I completed the whole process, from start to finish in one day. I felt great. My daughter did not feel like taking the time to glue her items on her page so she put the items where she wanted them and left her page on our kitchen counter. Well, since this counter was in a heavy traffic area, when we walked by sometimes her words would blow off her page or just move out of place.

After a few days of us stopping and taking the time to put her items back in their place, my daughter had an awesome idea. She took a picture of it with her cell phone, dismantled her page and put the paper away. Then she printed it. What a news flash for me, because up until that moment, for 25 years, I had been taking over an hour to glue everything on my page. Needless to say, now I take pictures of my pages, create various versions, and print the page I like best. Then I frame them, except if I'm using canvas.

Regardless what method, background or technique you choose, once you complete your image page or vision board, you must have it in a place where you can see it every day.

Remember, repetition is the key. Your brain must be exposed to the board regularly in order for it to influence your consciousness into moving into the direction of your intentions. Vision boards are powerful influences on the brain because they work on both the left and right sides of your brain. The words hit the left side of the brain. The pictures and images work on the right side of the brain. And don't forget, the RAS in the brain will kick in, because you targeted new things that are relevant to you and your life now.

Basically, you are programming your brain much the way you see in billboards when you see them by the road, or the way you see advertisements when you are watching TV and commercials come on. Advertisers study consumer behavior and they know what colors and what images grab our attention, and what sounds, songs and jingles condition our brains to buy certain products and services. The repetition of being exposed to the same billboards, for the few seconds that you see them when you are driving by, and repetition of exposure to TV commercials influence your belief systems, your choices, and not to forget your RAS.

So I say, rather than living your life by making a lot of choices that you were conditioned/programmed to make by companies, and advertisers, live your life making choices from which you condition or program your own brain. Don't float in the wind or be a puppet on a string. Get in the driver's seat! Program/Rewire your own brain.

Chapter 27

Meditation

Practicing meditation can help you rewire your brain. There are numerous published studies that go into detail about the many benefits of how meditation can improve our lives. Since my purpose in connecting with you is to provide information in a simplified and easy to implement manner, I will not go the scientific "wordy" route of discussing, in detail, how meditation can help you to rewire your brain. I will say that science is just beginning to understand how meditation impacts the mind and body.

If you're interested, there is a ton of information out there for you to explore. If you don't know how to meditate, not to worry, because you can learn. There are many books, internet articles and YouTube tutorials on how to meditate. If you have a difficult time meditating, you can create an affirmation about meditation to help. It can be something as simple as: "Each and every day, my mind and my body become more and more receptive to meditation."

Remember, your RAS will be behind the scenes facilitating your process, influencing your brain and your body to embrace meditation. I like to meditate with meditation music or Reiki music playing in the background. Some people find it easier to meditate by using guided meditation (you can find these on YouTube).

In preparation for meditation, what's most important for you to do is to make sure that you will have uninterrupted time in a space where you are unlikely to be interrupted. Once you have your time and space, you are ready to roll. Your time for meditation can vary. You can start at 5 minutes, graduate to 10 minutes and up to 1 hour or more if you choose. Don't be hard on yourself if you cannot stay still for 5 minutes. Meditation is a practice that you have to develop.

We live in a world that has so much going on, constantly attracting our attention, especially in Western civilization. We get used to focusing on things outside of ourselves, and meditation is about going within. What would be helpful for you is to pick the same time and the same place to meditate daily. This way your brain and body will get programmed to be still at this time. Hence, you will rewire your brain to be still and quiet at a certain time every day, as opposed to your brain being focused on whatever habits you have going on now. I like to meditate in the morning before I say hello to the world.

Starting my day with meditation sets the tone for my day. I first start with a gratitude prayer and then I smoothly go into meditation. Different strokes for different folks. You have to find what works for you. So, practice, practice, practice, so you can find your groove.

I have developed a morning ritual of focusing on my affirmations and vision boards after I open my eyes from my 30-minute to one-hour meditation.

During this time, the theta brainwave cycle is activated. Brain waves are basically synchronized electrical pulses in the brain. There are alpha waves and delta waves, but theta brainwaves are significant. There is an indication that theta brainwave cycles are really good for programming/rewiring the brain. Science reveals that young children's brains mostly operate in the theta brainwave cycles, and alpha cycles; between the ages of 1 year old to 6 years old young children have to take in a whole lot of information about how their world/environment operates so that they can function. They are like recorders with the record button pushed, or like sponges soaking up information, or little computers getting downloads and downloads of programs.

Hence, since young children's brains are naturally in the theta cycle during a significant time in their lives wherein, they must download a lot of programs, it follows that we can more easily download programs when our brainwaves are in the theta cycle, as well.

Of course, repetition is the key. When I open my eyes after 30 minutes to one hour of meditation, my brainwaves are in the theta cycle primed for my programming/rewiring process. This is when I do my thing with my vision boards and affirmations.

I want to mention that when I am in the theta zone, I feel oneness with the universe. I do not even feel the presence of my body; I am aligned with my self-as-consciousness. In addition, I don't feel separation from my goals on my vision boards and affirmations. I feel good. It's like they already exist, perhaps in an alternate reality. Oops, I dropped off into the rabbit hole again. So here we go.

You have probably heard that physicists have theories about the existence of other dimensions, and that everything is going on at the same time ("past, present and future"), and that time is a concept that is relative and not fixed. Here, I want to mention that I have had personal experiences that revealed other dimensions and time being relative. No, I'm not crazy. I'm speaking of my out-of-body experience (OBE) in the astral dimension (I was totally conscious during my experience).

I have also had experience with remote viewing, which you can look up if you're interested. Furthermore, almost 30 years ago, I was guided by my "future self" to get me to where I am now. During that journey, I eventually merged with that part of myself and became that self, which was the next highest version of myself. I recently heard a term for this called "quantum jumping," which means being able to communicate with a version of yourself that has already done what you are trying to do. I must say that I have had some experiences that definitely let me know that there is more to "beingness" than what meets our five senses.

Back to meditation, though. Practicing meditation will enhance your life. You can practice meditation to enhance your physical body and your mental, emotional and spiritual well-being. Meditation can help you to rewire your brain. So come on, get started. The clock is ticking…although time isn't real but is relative. Level up! Rewire your brain.

Chapter 28

Visualization

Practicing visualization can also help you to rewire your brain. To practice visualization, you need to create the same conditions as you would for meditation. You need uninterrupted time and space. Before you go into your visualization, focus on your affirmations and vision boards. This will help to put you in the mindset of what to visualize. Also, as you focus on your vision boards, imagine that everything on the board is happening right here, right now. What does that look like for you?

Allow yourself to actually feel all of the "feel-good" emotions that come along with your having accomplished your desires. Smile, say "yes!" Then, slowly, while sitting in a comfortable position, close your eyes. Relax. Slowly Inhale and exhale as you envision your experience. Imagine yourself doing those things that you want to do, being in those places that you want to be, being that person whom you want to become, the next highest version of yourself. See and open yourself up to the new you! Your brain does not know the difference between what is real and what is not real. It will give you an emotional experience relative to whatever you focus on. Feel good. Smile. Enjoy. Rewire your brain.

Chapter 29

Mindfulness

Practicing mindfulness can help you rewire your brain because it puts you in touch with yourself and your inner world. Mindfulness is about awareness. Mindfulness is being aware in the present moment. Have you ever eaten your food so fast that you didn't really taste it, you didn't savor the flavor? You ate because it was something you needed to do so that you could attend to your next move. Have you ever driven home and when you got there you realized that your mind was somewhere else, while your car drove you home?

Have you ever missed your exit because you weren't paying attention? Have you ever said something inappropriate, or let something come out of your mouth without thinking? All of the above situations are examples of not being mindful, of not being aware in your present moment.

A lot of times, during my sessions with clients, I will ask them what thoughts are in their head, and they say that they don't know. I can tell that there is something going on because of the shifts in their facial expressions, body language, or breathing. Yet they are not aware of the thoughts running through their brains. I teach them mindfulness exercises to increase their awareness. Fortunately, there are a lot of mindfulness exercises and tutorials online. Explore and find what works for you and practice them regularly.

Well, how can mindfulness help me rewire my brain? Great question, and I'm glad you asked. Remember earlier when I discussed identifying habits, discerning thoughts, and triggers? You will not be able to do any of the work to rewire your brain if you are not aware of, for example, when your bad habit kicks in and you are supposed to instantly implement your new habit.

Awareness is a *must* to create change in your life. You have to be aware of when you are focusing on stinkin' thinkin' so that you can implement strategies to deter your focus and eventually deactivate the habit of focusing on negativity. Awareness is also a must when working to download the habit of focusing on healthy and productive thoughts.

Mindfulness exercises

*Mindful breathing- Inhale to the count of five, hold it to the count of five, then exhale to the count five. Do this 5 consecutive times.

* Senses exercise

-Look around your environment and say at least three things that you are aware of seeing

    I am aware of seeing the shadow on the wall.

    I am aware of seeing the pillow on the couch.

    I am aware of seeing my foot on the floor.

-Pay attention to sounds and say at least three things that you are aware of hearing

    I am aware of hearing the clock ticking.

    I am aware of hearing someone talking.

    I am aware of hearing a flute in that music.

-Pay attention to things that you are feeling (bodily sensations) and say three of them

    I am aware of feeling the pressure of my back on the chair.

    I am aware of feeling my hair on my forehead.

    I am aware of feeling my scarf around my neck.

Bring awareness to what you are thinking, doing and sensing in your life. Practice mindfulness. Mindfulness will help you to rewire your brain.

Chapter 30

Reinterpreting Your Past

If you want change, you don't have to take that long journey back into your past, dwelling there and trying to figure out why you are the way you are. Some reflection is good; just don't dwell in your past. While I'm sure that "pasting" would be an interesting journey, it will take a lot of time for you to go back into your past and you could have spent a lot of that time moving forward into the new you. All of your power is in your now moment. All of your power is in the present.

What power am I talking about? I'm glad you asked. I'm talking about the power to consciously choose change. Any time you spend dipping back into your past would be better spent if you were reinterpreting the past. Here I'm talking about "negative" situations from your past. When you reinterpret your past productively, you unload baggage that weighs you down, that creates stress in your life. When you are reinterpreting your past, you are looking back, not actually going back to be knee deep in the doo-doo. You look back as an observer with the conscious intention of reinterpreting the past, putting a different, productive meaning on it.

If you go back and get knee deep in the doo-doo, then you will be wrapped up in your emotions, and we cannot think straight when we are in our emotions. When you can't think straight, you will not be in the highest mental state to reinterpret your past. It makes sense to be in a positive or productive space to create something positive or productive. In short, this is an explanation of the concept of reinterpreting your past.

When something happens in our life, we place a meaning on it: This happened, so it means that. To reinterpret that "something" that happened, we look at that "something" from a higher perspective and place a productive meaning on it. Because that "something" has already happened, it is in the past.

So when you reinterpret it, when you look at it from a higher perspective, hence, giving it new meaning, you have reinterpreted your past. I suggest reinterpreting your past, when your past has negative meaning for you. When you think about something in your past and you feel anxiety, fear, worry, anger, resentment, shame, or other uncomfortable emotions, this is prime past material for you to reinterpret.

Every obstacle is an opportunity for growth. We can turn our lemons into lemonade. We cannot change the past, but we can grow from it. To provide you with a couple of examples of reinterpreting the past, I'm going to refer to some tidbits from my past.

When I was a young child and a young adult, I used to believe that my mother did not love me because of her mentally and emotionally abusive ways. Here is how I reinterpreted my past as it related to my mother: My mother had unresolved childhood issues and likely some trauma. She did not get any mental health assistance. She drank alcohol to numb her pain. She was self-medicating. When she was under the influence, she said and did some mean and hurtful things to me and sometimes she did not remember these things. Hurt people, hurt people. She demonstrated her love to me by providing all of the things that I needed and most of the things that I wanted. She wanted to make sure that I had things that she did not have when she was growing up. She gave me what she could give. She loved me in the way that she knew how.

This reinterpretation is my current mindset, about my mother. It didn't happen overnight. I had to work on myself. I had to not allow myself to focus on the thoughts of my mother that were negative. When the negative thoughts popped into my head, I made myself focus on the reinterpreted version of my past repeatedly, until that mindset got wired into my brain.

Now, here is another short example of how I reinterpreted a different part of my past. My ex-husband was very abusive towards me. I used to believe that I was a helpless victim. How did I reinterpret that past? I learned that I am a powerful creator and that I made choices that led to my staying in that relationship and accepting the abuse.

One of the reasons that I stayed was because I wanted to turn that situation into the family situation that I desired, but to no avail. I eventually made the choice to leave, and I left. I could have made that choice at any time. Every woman has her reasons for staying in an unhealthy relationship. It is a choice. It is a choice to stay and it is a choice to leave, no matter how difficult the leaving might be. We have the freedom of choice. We are so free that we can choose victimhood.

Chapter 31

Identify and Change Your Programs

Another way of creating positive change when looking back at your past is to identify your negative programs and change them. Anytime you are talking about an experience that you have already had -- an experience that has nothing to do with your current moment -- you are talking about the past, or maybe you are thinking about the past. Nevertheless, you are focused on the past. To create positive change, when you reflect back into your past, look for those negative programs that you have running in that brain of yours that you want to deactivate.

To gauge positive change and growth, look for those programs that are not bringing you what you want in life. Write them down: "I'm not good enough," "I'm not worthy," "I don't deserve to be happy." Whatever your negative programs are, identify them. Write them down. Once you have your list, you can read one negative program and come up with a productive program that you want to replace it with. Then, you read another program, and identify a productive program that you want to replace that one with. Continue this process until you have a productive replacement program for all of your negative programs.

Now, you are ready for the next step. As you practice mindfulness, in your daily life, when you notice one of your negative programs running (your RAS will help with this), consciously make yourself say, think or do your new, positive program that you wrote on your list. When you do this over and over again, because repetition is the key, you will have created your new program that will activate when the trigger shows up. Be persistent and determined. Work it, work it, work it. Rewire your brain.

Chapter 32

How Long Will It Take to Rewire My Brain?

Good question. Science is not sure of the exact amount of time it will take to rewire your brain. There are factors to take into consideration, such as how long you have had the negative programs and habits. If you have had a habit for 30 years, and another habit for one year, it would seem that the one-year habit will be easier to change/deactivate. And then there is the consideration of how frequently you work your program. If you have a one-year habit that you want to change, but you only work your program once a week, then that bad habit is going to be around for a while.

Another consideration could be that your belief systems anchor your behavioral habits in place. I will share a personal example that comes to mind: My mother was born in 1929. Her era was the Great Depression era. The financial market crashed in the United States and around the globe and money was tight. People sometimes did not know where their next meal was coming from.

How did the Great Depression impact my mother? My mother used to keep things that she could have thrown away. When I was growing up, my mother used to keep a lot of "almost empty" containers such as dishwashing liquid, detergent for clothes, and cleaning solutions under the kitchen sink. She kept them so we would have those products if we ran out. She had certain sayings like "Money don't grow on trees," so she was keeping all of that stuff for that "rainy day" that she always talked about. Well, that "rainy day" never came because my mother had a good job at the automobile plant with my uncles, making the good money that they made back in the day. Even though her life circumstances had changed since the Great Depression, she still held onto beliefs about that "rainy day" when there might not be enough money to take care of all the things that she needed to take care of.

Because the Great Depression was a serious time of survival, her belief system about money anchored her "saving things" behavior in place. Because I was raised by her, I adopted some of those same habits just from watching her and also being taught by her about money and the lack of it. I didn't even notice that I had picked up her habit until I was an adult and a friend of mine looked under my kitchen sink and asked me why I had so many "almost" empty containers. I realized that I got that habit from my mother.

When I embarked upon my journey of change, I realized that I didn't have to save "almost" empty containers anymore. So I practiced emptying contents into a different container and throwing away the rest of the bottles. I didn't have the Great Depression experience of survival loaded into my consciousness, so that container situation was a behavioral habit that was easier for me to break/deactivate than it would have been for my mother. When I happen across other things that I had been saving, those things that were out of sight, out of mind, I practice letting go of those things, as well.

It is like a double whammy when you have a habitual behavior that is anchored by a belief system. Remember that a belief system is basically thoughts that you focused on repeatedly, over and over, until it turned into a habitual way of perceiving something. Sometimes, the thoughts are not based in reality, but nevertheless, they are still part of your belief system. Hence a belief system is a habit. If you have two habits supporting each other I would recommend changing your mindset (belief system) as you simultaneously work on changing your behavior.

In the case of my mother's Great Depression consciousness, if she had only worked on emptying the containers and throwing things away (behavioral habit), she would have experienced a lot of fear because her keeping the containers represented an element of safety.

The fear would not have allowed her to continue throwing things away, "putting herself in jeopardy" (even if there is no real threat of jeopardy). Remember, the brain does not know the difference between what is real and what is not real. It signals emotions that match the thoughts you focus on.

If you have a similar situation wherein your habitual behavior is strongly connected to a belief system rooted in survival, it will be important for you to let your brain know that you are safe. Of course, if you are not safe don't try to convince your brain that you are. If you are not in any danger, you can simply repeat, aloud or silently, this mantra, "I am safe," or, "I will be, okay." Eventually, you will feel more relaxed and at ease. If you have experienced trauma, psychotherapy or the "tapping" intervention might be a route to consider. Tapping combines principles of modern psychology and Chinese acupressure for stress relief.

When it comes to rewiring your brain, remember that repetition is the key. As for how long it should take, you should notice some change in 30 days if you implement several strategies, at least twice a day. Strategies include: Affirmations; vision boards; visualization, and mindfulness. You also need to continue to engage in the desired behavior when the undesired habit is triggered, and do not allow yourself to engage in stinkin' thinkin'. You are a powerful being. You are capable of creating the change that you desire. Practice, Practice, Practice. Rewire your brain.

Chapter 33

Positive Support System

If you are planning to do a major brain rewiring overhaul like I had to do, it is important for you to have a support system. Your support system can be a friend, family member, social media group, mentor, co-worker, or therapist. It can be anyone who has your best interests at heart, someone who is for your highest good, who supports your desire and efforts to grow, to level up.

Having support is significant, because the process of rewiring your brain is about stepping outside your comfort zone. And if you're in for a major overhaul, you will be living outside your comfort zone, at least until the rewiring is successful, at which point you will have created a new comfort zone/program.

When we are outside our comfort zones, anxiety will emerge. Remember that the brain is about survival; it does not know if you will survive doing this new thing you are working on, but it knows you will survive with your current habit because you are still alive and continuously engage in your current habits. If you experience anxiety, don't focus on the anxiety-provoking thoughts, instead tell yourself that anxiety is normal because you are outside your comfort zone and you are growing, making positive changes, rewiring your brain.

Your support system, by being your cheerleader and witness, can keep you anchored in the truth of what you are doing, which is making positive, productive changes in your life. Your support system will encourage you to keep moving forward and will remind you of your ability to consciously rewire your brain. In addition, your support system will be sharing with you the progress that you are making and the progress that you have made.

If your support system has had experience in the brain rewiring process, even better, because they can offer feedback that other people won't be able to offer. Sometimes your support system will be the wind beneath your wings, as you learn how to fly. My best friend and spiritual sister, Godis, of over 30 years has been the wind beneath my wings, plenty of times, before I learned how to fly.

When I was stifled by my mental and emotional bondage, she saw in me more than I saw in myself. She saw strength in me when I saw weakness. She saw courage when I saw fear. She encouraged and supported me to keep moving forward. She pointed out the growth in my development, mentally, emotionally, and spiritually. I began to believe that I could become the highest version of myself. My readiness for change increased significantly. I was pregnant with the desire of giving birth to my new Self.

Godis was like a midwife and she was also my witness. She was there with me through my "birthing pains," my tears, and my fears. The fruits of my labor began to manifest. I began to feel inner peace, joy, happiness, courage, strength, and confidence. I began to feel a greater sense of love for myself and appreciation for life. My ability to manifest the things that I wanted became stronger. I had the attitude of gratitude. I experienced a deeper and more intimate relationship with The Creator. I was transformed. My mind had been made new.

I rewired my brain and ultimately gave birth to my Higher Self. I broke free from my chains of bondage and triumphantly stepped into a better life. The wonderful thing is, all of what Godis did for me, I did for her, as well. We were mastermind partners. We shared our affirmations, we visualized them together. We affirmed and proclaimed each other's success in the present moment before it had even happened. She used to always say, see those things as you would have them be as if they already are.

As a result of our dedication to investing our time and energy into our growth and development, we learned how to consciously create a new reality, by consistently giving focus to what we wanted to experience. To this day, we still mastermind, sharing ideas, and Godis continues to be a midwife, assisting other women with giving birth to the highest vision of themselves.

I encourage you to get started today. Reach out to others. There is someone, or maybe even a group somewhere, who would love to support your growth.

You can start your own "Rewire Your Brain" group if you know enough people who would like to work on changing for the best. Everyone can get a book, and you can work on reading and discussing chapters at a time. An extra bonus would be if everyone had the workbook to this book, and the group shared chapter by chapter from the workbook and supported each other in their process of growth. However, you decide to do it, get started! Identify your support system. Rewire your brain.

PS: If there is someone, or some people in your life who do not support your growth, don't try and force them to. We cannot change anyone. We can only change our self. Forge ahead. Find a support system and rewire your brain. Support can also be found in the spiritual realm, through God, angels, saints, ancestors, and spiritual beliefs and practices. You choose who you want to flow with.

PSS: As you change, sometimes the people in your life change. Everything is energy vibrating at a different frequency. You are an energy being. As your thoughts/programs change, you change and you vibrate at a different frequency. When you start vibrating at a different frequency, you don't "vibe" with some people in the same way that you vibed before. Sometimes, people drift apart. Some people come into your life for a season and a reason, and some people come and stay for a lifetime. Nevertheless, you keep moving forward. Rewire your brain.

Chapter 34

Conscious Effort: Investing Your Time and Energy Into Yourself

In order for you to rewire your brain, you really have to have a strong desire to feel good, and to be happy. Otherwise, you will likely give up before you complete the rewiring process. In addition, you have to be willing to let go, to not hold on to thoughts, beliefs, or behaviors that will inhibit your forward movement. For example, on my path of rewiring my brain, I identified affirmations about being happy, and having inner peace.

After all the hell that I had gone through in my life, I needed relief. I needed a new way of being in the world. Well, guess what? When I embarked upon the path of happiness and inner peace, I was met with some hurdles. What kind of hurdles? I'm glad you asked. Imagine this: I experienced a significant amount of abuse perpetrated against me by my ex-husband. Because of my being abused, you might think that it was justified for me to stay upset with my ex-husband. However, holding onto anger, resentment, and blame is not on the path of happiness or peace, so my hurdle was that I had to be willing to let go, and see him in a different light, to see him through the lenses of compassion and love.

So I could have either held on to and focused on thoughts about how wrong he was for abusing me and what a bad husband he was for doing the things he did to me, or I could make a conscious choice to see something different, something more productive.

Because I really, really, really, really wanted to be happy, and to experience inner peace, I made the conscious choice to do my inner work to jump over that hurdle so that I could continue my journey on the path of love and peace. I engaged in lots of prayer and meditation and I followed my inner guidance system to be able to make it over that hurdle. I had to learn how to forgive, give forth my anger, resentment, and the blame. In my process, I learned that forgiveness is not something that you do, it is what happens once you understand. I came to understand that my ex-husband entered this world as a baby, just as I did. His brain got programmed by his environment and everything and everyone in it, just like mine did. He was operating from his programs just like I was. And he was valuable and worthy of love just like me. I gained compassion for him, while still keeping a healthy distance from him, relationship-wise. I co-parented with him as best I could. I learned that although I could not control anyone else, I could learn to control myself. Hence, no matter how he behaved in the co-parenting encounters, I had the ability to control myself. It was a challenge for me to learn to practice a different way of being in our interactions.

I had to learn to not be reactive; I had to work on my triggers in order to be successful with this one. I had to learn to say and do productive things. I had to learn to sometimes not say anything at all. When I changed, the dynamics in the relationship changed. You see, people operate from habits/programs in relationships. One person does this, then the other person does that. It's like a dance that occurs to the music of life. Well, if one person changes their dance moves, then the dance between the two of them has to change. Before, it looked like this. And now it looks like that. Every time someone changes a habit in a relationship, that change has an effect on the relationship.

It is important to note that oftentimes people treat you the way you treat yourself. If you don't value yourself, they might not value you either. But getting back to my relationship/co-parenting with my ex-husband, as time went on, and I was consciously working on myself and rewiring my brain, the dynamics of our relationship shifted significantly.

It was not an overnight process to be certain, but currently, my ex-husband and I have a very good relationship. I changed, he changed. Now, we laugh, we talk and we enjoy family gatherings with our children and grandchildren. We even worked on and completed a CD together with him creating the music and me writing poetic lyrics and doing the vocals. The name of our CD is *From Sexual Energy to Love*. And get this, the lyrics are from a book that I wrote with the same title, *From Sexual Energy to Love*, and the lyrics are about romantic and loving experiences that I had with other men. My ex-husband and I both love our CD.

To this day, we both ride around in our vehicles listening to our own music. My favorite song is *Last Night*. I love it. Our relationship reflects the epitome of healing/changing the program. Every obstacle is an opportunity for growth! You've got this. Make it happen. Rewire your brain.

www.ingramcontent.com/pod-product-compliance
Lightning Source LLC
Chambersburg PA
CBHW030152100526
44592CB00009B/241